OPPENHEIMER

OPPENHEIMER

screenplay by
CHRISTOPHER NOLAN

based on the book
American Prometheus:
The Triumph and Tragedy of J. Robert Oppenheimer
by
KAI BIRD
and MARTIN J. SHERWIN

faber

First published in 2023
by Faber & Faber Limited
The Bindery, 51 Hatton Garden
London ECIN 8HN

First published in the USA in 2023

Typeset by Brighton Gray

A CIP record for this book is available from the British Library

ISBN 978-0-571-38131-9

4 6 8 10 9 7 5 3

Contents

Introduction

Robert Oppenheimer was always an enigma, even to his closest friends. As a troubled, socially awkward young man, he plumbed the mysteries of quantum physics. But he also loved the poetry of John Donne and read the *Bhagavad Gita* in the original Sanskrit. He was an aesthete who cultivated ambiguities in his own life. A Renaissance man, he brought together poetry and science. He was both brilliant and naive, insightful and terribly vulnerable. As his fellow physicist Isidor Rabi once remarked, in addition to being 'very wise, he was very foolish'.[1]

'In Oppenheimer,' Rabi wrote, 'the element of earthiness was feeble. Yet it was essentially this spiritual quality, this refinement as expressed in speech and manner, that was the basis of his charisma. He never expressed himself completely. He always left a feeling that there were depths of sensibility and insight not yet revealed.'[2]

This was the complex man who led the effort in the midst of a world war to unleash the power of the atom. The 'father' of the atomic bomb was painfully aware of the moral consequences. He had dedicated his life to science and rational thought. And yet, his decision to join in the creation of a genocidal weapon was, in the words of the physicist Freeman Dyson, 'a Faustian bargain if there ever was one . . . And of course we are still living with it.'[3]

Oppenheimer's story reminds us that our identity as human beings is now forever intimately connected with the culture of things nuclear. This is particularly true for citizens of the country that used the first atomic bomb on two Japanese cities. 'We have had the bomb on our minds since 1945,' wrote the novelist E. L. Doctorow. 'It was first our weaponry and then our diplomacy, and now it's our economy. How can we suppose that something so monstrously powerful would not, after forty years, compose our identity? The great golem we have made against our enemies is our culture, our bomb culture – its logic, its faith, its vision.'[4]

Christopher Nolan's brilliant film *Oppenheimer* is based on the 2005 biography *American Prometheus: The Triumph and Tragedy of J. Robert Oppenheimer.* The book was a quarter-century in the making. My late co-author, Martin J. Sherwin, signed the contract with Knopf in 1980. Over the years, he interviewed nearly a hundred of Oppenheimer's friends, students, relatives and colleagues, most of whom are now dead. The biography also draws on some 50,000 pages of archival materials from all over the world, including Oppenheimer's own massive collection of papers at the Library of Congress, and some 8,000 pages of FBI records accumulated over twenty-five years of surveillance. Few men in public life have been subjected to such scrutiny by the authorities; Oppenheimer's words were captured on tape by FBI recording devices and transcribed. All of these sources gave his biographers the opportunity to create a rich and authoritative narrative.

In the year 2000, when Marty Sherwin invited me to join him on his long biographical journey, we sealed the deal by raising our martini glasses and Marty intoned Oppenheimer's favoured toast, 'To the confusion of our enemies.' Marty then remarked that Oppenheimer's life was much larger than just the story of his building the atomic bomb. He was America's Prometheus, the Greek god who stole fire from Zeus and gave it to humans. And like Prometheus, Oppenheimer had led the effort to wrest from nature the awesome fire of the sun for his country in a time of war. But like Prometheus, Oppenheimer was later punished. 'We would not be spending so much time and effort on this biography,' Sherwin told me, 'if Oppenheimer had not been humiliated in the 1954 security hearing. It is the travesty of the trial that makes the arc for the story.'

Nolan's screenplay artfully captures this narrative as told in *American Prometheus,* the triumphant story of Los Alamos and the Manhattan Project – but also focusing on the tragedy of Oppenheimer's downfall.

In the dark days of the early 1950s, Oppenheimer became the most prominent victim of America's McCarthyite witch-hunt. In 1954, just nine years after he was feted as the 'father of the atomic bomb', Oppenheimer was put on trial in a kangaroo court proceeding – just as another scientist, Galileo Galilei, had been tried and humiliated by a medieval-minded church in Rome in 1633.

Soon after Hiroshima, he began speaking out about the dangers of the atom bomb. In October 1945 he astonished one audience by saying that the Hiroshima bomb had been used 'against an essentially defeated enemy . . . it is a weapon for aggressors, and the elements of surprise and terror are as intrinsic to it as are the fissionable nuclei.'[5]

His fate was sealed when he blurted out to President Harry Truman, 'I feel I have blood on my hands.'[6] Upon which, Truman dismissed him from the Oval Office, telling his aides that he didn't want to see that 'crybaby scientist' ever again. But just a few years later, Oppenheimer spoke out repeatedly against the building of the even more destructive hydrogen bomb. This earned him other powerful enemies, in particular, the animosity of Lewis Strauss, the chairman of the Atomic Energy Commission.

It was Strauss who then orchestrated the security hearing trial that questioned Oppenheimer's loyalty and ultimately stripped him of his security clearance. In the conduct of the trial, the Atomic Energy Commission violated its own regulations for a security review. Among a long list of transgressions, they illegally wiretapped Oppenheimer's home and the office of his lawyer. Nothing incriminating was discovered. They allowed the three-member security panel access to Oppenheimer's 8,000-page FBI file – but denied his own lawyer security clearance to read the material being used selectively against his client. They blackmailed otherwise friendly witnesses to turn against Oppenheimer. It was a travesty. And then Strauss leaked the entire transcript of the hearing to the *New York Times*.

Oppenheimer became a pariah, 'defrocked in his own church', in the words of yet another adversary, the physicist Edward Teller. Oppenheimer was deeply wounded. He spent the rest of his life as a political non-entity. Upon his death from oesophageal cancer in 1967, Senator J. William Fulbright went to the floor of the Senate and said, 'Let us remember not only what his special genius did for us; let us also remember what we did to him.'[7]

Nolan's screenplay should ignite a national discussion about our nuclear history. Perhaps in anticipation of the film, the US government finally revisited the 1954 trial, and in December 2022 the *New York Times* ran a long story reporting that Secretary of Energy Jennifer Granholm had 'nullified a 1954 decision to revoke the security clearance of J. Robert Oppenheimer, a top government scientist who led the making of the atomic bomb in World War II but fell under suspicion of being a Soviet spy at the height of the McCarthy era.'[8] Secretary Granholm explained that her department had been 'entrusted with the responsibility to correct the historical record and honour Dr Oppenheimer's profound contributions to our national defence and scientific enterprise at large'.

Secretary Granholm's decision officially corrects the historical record. This lesson is particularly important because of Oppenheimer's status as a scientist. We are a society immersed in science and technology, some of it based on the very physics that Oppenheimer and his colleagues pioneered. And yet many in the US still distrust science and scientists.

In some discernable measure, we can blame the legacy of the flawed Oppenheimer security trial for this distrust. In 1954, America's most celebrated scientist was falsely accused and publicly humiliated, sending a warning to all scientists not to engage in the political arena as public intellectuals. This was the real tragedy of Oppenheimer. What happened to him damaged our ability as a society to debate honestly about scientific theory – the very foundation of our modern world.

*

Christopher Nolan's screenplay is an extraordinarily creative achievement. Oppenheimer's iconic life is no ordinary story. I only wish that my collaborator, Martin J. Sherwin, was still with us. He died in October 2021 at the age of eighty-four, just days before Nolan announced to the world that he had sold his screenplay to Universal Studios. Marty knew about the project, but he never had a chance to read the screenplay, let alone see the film. But he knew full well how formidable a challenge it was to take a 722-page biography and turn it into a transformative film. He knew that more than one screenwriter had tried and failed to do the same. He would have been excited and gratified to read this script. And I think the biographer in him would have appreciated how well Nolan has taken an extremely complicated life story and miraculously turned it into visual art that is faithful both to the history and the man.

KAI BIRD
March 2023

Notes

1. Bird & Sherwin, *American Prometheus*, p. 5.
2. Bird & Sherwin, *American Prometheus*, p. 588.
3. Bird & Sherwin, *American Prometheus*, p. 5.
4. Bird & Sherwin, *American Prometheus*, p. xii.
5. Bird & Sherwin, *American Prometheus*, p. 324.
6. Bird & Sherwin, *American Prometheus*, p. 332.
7. Bird & Sherwin, *American Prometheus*, p. 588.
8. William J. Broad, 'Architect of Atomic Bomb Cleared of "Black Mark"', *NYT*, Dec. 18, 2022.

*

Kai Bird is the Executive Director of the Leon Levy Center for Biography in New York City. He and Martin J. Sherwin won the Pulitzer Prize in 2006 for their biography, American Prometheus: The Triumph and Tragedy of J. Robert Oppenheimer.

Cast and Credits

CILLIAN MURPHY
EMILY BLUNT
MATT DAMON
ROBERT DOWNEY JR.
FLORENCE PUGH
JOSH HARTNETT
CASEY AFFLECK

with
RAMI MALEK
and
KENNETH BRANAGH

BENNY SAFDIE
JASON CLARKE

DYLAN ARNOLD
TOM CONTI
JAMES D'ARCY

DAVID DASTMALCHIAN
DANE DEHAAN
ALDEN EHRENREICH

TONY GOLDWYN
JEFFERSON HALL
DAVID KRUMHOLTZ
MATTHEW MODINE

A Universal Pictures
presentation

A Syncopy
production

In association with
Atlas Entertainment

A Film by
CHRISTOPHER NOLAN

OPPENHEIMER

Based on the Book
American Prometheus:
The Triumph and Tragedy of J. Robert Oppenheimer
by
KAI BIRD *and* MARTIN J. SHERWIN

Written for the Screen and Directed by	CHRISTOPHER NOLAN
Produced by	EMMA THOMAS P.G.A.
Produced by	CHARLES ROVEN P.G.A.
Produced by	CHRISTOPHER NOLAN P.G.A.
Executive Producers	J. DAVID WARGO
	JAMES WOODS
Executive Producer	THOMAS HAYSLIP
Director of Photography	HOYTE VAN HOYTEMA, ASC, FSF, NSC
Production Designer	RUTH DE JONG
Edited by	JENNIFER LAME, ACE
Music by	LUDWIG GÖRANSSON
Visual Effects Supervisor	ANDREW JACKSON
Special Effects Supervisor	SCOTT FISHER
Costumes Designed by	ELLEN MIROJNICK
Co-Producer	ANDY THOMPSON
Casting by	JOHN PAPSIDERA CSA

OPPENHEIMER

THE SCREENPLAY

A VAST SPHERE OF FIRE, the fire of a thousand suns, slowly eats the night-time desert. A line of black type appears:

'Prometheus stole fire from the Gods and gave it to man.'

And the sound of DOZENS OF FEET STAMPING RHYTHMICALLY . . .

'For this he was chained to a rock and tortured for eternity.'

ROILING PLASMA expands, the sound of STAMPING GROWS OPPRESSIVE, the STAMPING FASTER and FASTER over –

A FACE. Gaunt, tense. EYES TIGHTLY SHUT. The face SHUDDERS – the sound CEASES as my EYES OPEN, STARING INTO CAMERA:

Peer into my soul – J. ROBERT OPPENHEIMER, aged fifty, close-cropped greying hair. The gentle sounds of bureaucracy . . .

SUPER TITLE:

'I. FISSION'

> VOICE
> (O.S.)
> Dr Oppenheimer, as we begin, I believe you have a statement to read into the record?

I glance down at my notes.

> OPPENHEIMER
> Yes, your honour –

> SECOND VOICE
> (O.S.)
> We're not judges, doctor.

> OPPENHEIMER
> No. Of course.

(I start reading)
Members of the Security Board, the so-called derogatory
information in your indictment of me cannot be fairly
understood except in the context of my life and my work.
This answer is a summary of relevant aspects of my life in
more or less chronological order . . .

SENATE AIDE
(V.O.)
How long did he testify?

Cut to:

INT. SENATE OFFICE – DAY (BLACK-AND-WHITE
SEQUENCE)

Close on a prosperous sixty-three-year-old man, LEWIS STRAUSS,
as he takes a cup of coffee from a SENATE AIDE . . .

SUPER TITLE:

'2. FUSION'

STRAUSS
*I forget. Three days, or so. The whole hearing took a
month.*

SENATE AIDE
An ordeal.

STRAUSS
*I've only read the transcript, but who'd want to justify
their whole life?*

SENATE AIDE
You weren't there?

STRAUSS
*As Chairman, I wasn't allowed to be. Are they really going
to ask about it? It was years ago.*

SENATE AIDE

Four years ago. Oppenheimer still divides America – the Committee will want to know where you stood.
                    (checks his watch)
Ready?

INT. CORRIDOR, SENATE BUILDING – MOMENTS LATER
(B & W)

The Senate Aide leads Strauss along the corridor.

SENATE AIDE

Senator Thurmond asked me to say not to feel you're on trial.

STRAUSS

I didn't, till you said that.

SENATE AIDE

Really, Mr Strauss –

STRAUSS

Admiral.

SENATE AIDE

Admiral Strauss, this is a formality. President Eisenhower's asked you to be in his Cabinet, the Senate really has no choice but to confirm you.

They arrive at the door.

STRAUSS

And if they bring up Oppenheimer?

SENATE AIDE

When they bring up Oppenheimer, answer honestly and no senator can deny that you did your duty. It'll be uncomfortable . . .
                    (smiles)
Who wants to justify their whole life?

5

The door to the VAST *committee room opens – they enter,* FLASHBULBS POPPING *as* PRESS *and* PUBLIC *see Strauss.*

> ROBB
> (V.O.)
> *Why did you leave the United States?*

Cut to:

INT. ROOM 2022, ATOMIC ENERGY COMMISSION – DAY (COLOUR)

The room is SMALL, SHABBY. Surprised, I look up from my statement at the prosecutor, Roger ROBB. Then turn to the THREE BOARD MEMBERS (GRAY, EVANS, MORGAN).

> OPPENHEIMER
> I wanted to learn the new physics.

> GRAY
> Was there nowhere here? I thought Berkeley had the leading theoretical physics department –

> OPPENHEIMER
> Sure. Once I built it. First I had to go to Europe. I went to Cambridge to work under Patrick Blackett.

> ROBB
> Were you happier there than in America?

INSERT CUT: A YOUNG ME (TWENTY-ONE) LIES IN BED STARING UP, CRYING . . . PARTICLES WITH THE VASTNESS OF STARS MOVE LIKE FIREFLIES . . .

> OPPENHEIMER
> No. I was homesick. Emotionally immature . . . troubled by visions of a hidden universe . . .

INT. LABORATORY, CAMBRIDGE – DAY

The YOUNG ME, frazzled demeanor, STRUGGLES with equipment.

                    OPPENHEIMER
                       (V.O.)
. . . useless in the lab.

I drop a beaker, it SHATTERS. PATRICK BLACKETT looks over,
FROWNING. He picks up an APPLE and takes a LARGE BITE.

                      BLACKETT
                  (through apple)
Christ, Oppenheimer, have you had any sleep? Start again.

                 YOUNG OPPENHEIMER
I need to go to the lecture.

                      BLACKETT
Why?

                 YOUNG OPPENHEIMER
                    (pleading)
It's Niels Bohr.

Blackett check his watch – starts packing up –

                      BLACKETT
Damn, *completely* forgot. Let's go.

I start to pack up with the other students.

                      BLACKETT
Not you. Finish coating those plates.

I clean up as Blackett and the other students leave – one leaves
an APPLE for Blackett – GREEN WITH STEM AND TINY LEAF.

I pause at a bottle: 'Potassium Cyanide' . . . CLUMSY HANDS
SHAKING, I draw CYANIDE into a syringe. I INJECT the apple . . .

EXT. QUADRANGLE, CAMBRIDGE – EVENING

I HURRY across the quad. A lonely figure.

                        BOHR
                       (V.O.)
Quantum physics isn't a step forward . . .

                         7

INT. LECTURE HALL, CAMBRIDGE – CONTINUOUS

I sneak into the back of the auditorium. Standing, SPELLBOUND, as NIELS BOHR, a charismatic Dane, lectures.

> BOHR
> . . . It's a new way to understand reality. Einstein's opened a door, now we're peering through, seeing a world *inside* our world . . . a world of energy and paradox that not everyone can accept . . .

I RAISE my hand to ask a question . . .

Cut to:

INT. SENATE COMMITTEE HEARING ROOM – DAY (B&W)

Strauss sits facing the Committee, COUNSEL *beside him,* PRESS, CAMERAS *and* PUBLIC *behind . . .*

> SENATOR McGEE
> *Admiral Strauss, I'm interested in your relationship with Dr J. Robert Oppenheimer. You met in 1947?*

> STRAUSS
> *Correct.*

> SENATOR McGEE
> *You were a commissioner of the Atomic Energy Commission?*

> STRAUSS
> *I was, but I met Robert in my capacity as board member of the Institute for Advanced Study at Princeton. After the war he was world-renowned – the great man of physics . . .*

EXT. INSTITUTE FOR ADVANCED STUDY, PRINCETON – DAY (B&W)

Strauss, younger, fifty-one, bustles out of the Institute –

STRAUSS
(V.O.)
. . . I was determined to get him to run the Institute.

*– to welcome the rail-thin figure of Oppenheimer (forty-three),
emerging from a TAXI in HAT and coat, PIPE in mouth. ICONIC.*

STRAUSS
Dr Oppenheimer, an honour.

OPPENHEIMER
Mr Strauss.

STRAUSS
It's pronounced 'straws'.

OPPENHEIMER
*'Oh-ppenheimer', 'aw-ppenheimer' – any way you say it
they know I'm Jewish.*

STRAUSS
*I'm a proud member of Temple Emmanuel – 'straws' is the
Southern pronunciation. Welcome to the Institute. I think
you could be very happy here.*

OPPENHEIMER
Oh?

STRAUSS
*Well, you'll love the commute – the position comes with
that house for you and your wife.*

Strauss points along an avenue of trees to Olden Manor . . .

STRAUSS
And your two children . . .

Oppenheimer nods as he follows Strauss into the Institute.

INT. INSTITUTE FOR ADVANCED STUDY, PRINCETON –
CONTINUOUS (B&W)

Strauss leads Oppenheimer through the Institute.

STRAUSS
I'm a great admirer of your work.

OPPENHEIMER
You're a physicist by training, Mr Strauss?

STRAUSS
No, I'm not trained in physics, or anything else. I'm a self-made man.

OPPENHEIMER
I can relate to that . . .

STRAUSS
Really?

OPPENHEIMER
(dry)
My father was one.

INT. PRESIDENT'S OFFICE, INSTITUTE FOR ADVANCED STUDY – MOMENTS LATER (B&W)

Strauss shows Oppenheimer into the well-appointed office.

STRAUSS
This would be your office.

Oppenheimer drifts to the windows – a LAWN rolls down to a POND. He spots a FIGURE – long grey hair poking from under his hat –

STRAUSS
I'm told he's there most afternoons.

The figure gently tosses a stone into the water.

STRAUSS
I've always wondered why you didn't involve him in the Manhattan Project.

Oppenheimer turns to Strauss, interested . . .

STRAUSS
The greatest scientific mind of our time?

OPPENHEIMER
*Of <u>his</u> time. Einstein published his Theory of Relativity
more than forty years ago, but never embraced the
quantum world it revealed.*

STRAUSS
'God doesn't play dice.'

OPPENHEIMER
Precisely. You never thought of studying physics formally?

STRAUSS
I had offers. But I chose to sell shoes.

OPPENHEIMER
Lewis Strauss was once a lowly shoe salesman?

STRAUSS
No. Just a shoe salesman.
        (opens the door)
I'll introduce you –

OPPENHEIMER
No need. I've known him for years.

Strauss, awkward, stays in the doorway and WATCHES . . .

From afar: as Oppenheimer approaches, Einstein's HAT BLOWS
off his head, unleashing a MESS OF GREY HAIR, *hat rolling across
the grass to where Oppenheimer* SCOOPS *it up, and we . . .*

Cut to:

INT. ROOM 2022, ATOMIC ENERGY COMMISSION –
DAY (COLOUR)

I flip a page. Continue reading my statement.

OPPENHEIMER
I struggled badly trying to visualize this new world . . .

INT. ROOMS AT CAMBRIDGE – DAY

The Young Me lies on the floor, STARING UP . . .

> OPPENHEIMER
> (V.O.)
> . . . you had to retool your mind to see things hovering just out of sight . . .

INSERT CUT: POINTS OF LIGHT MOVE LIKE SPARKS, BUT IN A WAVE.

> OPPENHEIMER
> (V.O.)
> . . . then you could unlock forces never before imagined . . .

I wipe TEARS from my eyes.

INSERT CUT: STARS. SPARKS FROM A CAMPFIRE. I PAT THE NOSE OF A HORSE IN THE DARKNESS AS I FEED IT AN APPLE.

I grow calm, my eyelids lowering . . .

INSERT CUT: AN APPLE – GREEN WITH A STEM AND A TINY LEAF . . .

I OPEN my eyes – JUMP out of bed – SCRAMBLE to dress –

EXT. QUADRANGLE, CAMBRIDGE – MOMENTS LATER

I RUN, DESPERATE, AGAINST the crowd –

INT. LABORATORY, CAMBRIDGE – DAY

I BURST in – Blackett LOOKS UP. ANOTHER MAN has his back to me. Between them on the workbench – the POISONED APPLE . . .

> BLACKETT
> You alright?

I nod, awkward, trying to control my BREATHING . . .

BLACKETT
Niels, meet J. Robert Oppenheimer.

The other man TURNS, offers his hand – Niels Bohr.

BOHR
What does the 'J' stand for?

BLACKETT
Nothing, apparently.

Bohr takes me in – this strange, BREATHLESS young man . . .

BOHR
You were at my lecture. You asked the only good question.

BLACKETT
Nobody's denying his insight. It's his labouratory skills that
leave a little to be desired.

YOUNG OPPENHEIMER
I heard you give the same lecture –

BOHR
At Harvard. And you asked the same question. Why ask
again?

YOUNG OPPENHEIMER
I hadn't liked your answer.

BOHR
Did you like it better yesterday?

YOUNG OPPENHEIMER
A lot.

BOHR
You can lift the rock without being ready for the snake
that's revealed. Now, it seems, you're ready.

Bohr picks up the POISONED APPLE from Blackett's desk . . .

BOHR
You don't enjoy the lab?

I shake my head. Bohr GESTICULATES with the apple as he
talks – I watch it bob around – a kitten following a ball of
string . . .

> BOHR
>
> Get out of Cambridge, with its beakers and potions. Go
> somewhere they'll let you think . . .
>> (assesses me)
>
> Gottingen.

> BLACKETT
>
> Born?

> BOHR
>
> Born. Get to Germany. Study under Max Born. Learn the
> ways of theory. I'll send word.

Bohr raises the apple to take a bite – I GRAB it –

> YOUNG OPPENHEIMER
>
> Wormhole.

– DROP it into the wastebasket. Blackett peers at it, curious.

> BOHR
>
> How's your mathematics?

> BLACKETT
>
> Not good enough for the physicist he wants to be.

> BOHR
>
> Algebra's like sheet music. The important thing isn't can
> you read music, it's can you *hear* it. Can you hear the
> music, Robert?

> YOUNG OPPENHEIMER
>
> I can.

SPARKS explode in WAVES, WAVES of FIRE CRASHING on a SHORE
of GLASS, FLYING OVER the MEDIEVAL SPIRES of Gottingen,
I watch BORN and BOHR and DIRAC, GALAXIES of PARTICLES
DISPERSE and REFORM, a CUBIST PAINTING transfixes the
Young Me, an ORCHESTRA plays STRAVINSKY, I read THE WASTE

LAND, I WRITE FURIOUSLY at a desk, I WRITE FURIOUSLY on a chalkboard, I SMASH a glass, and ANOTHER, and ANOTHER, WATCHING the SHARDS skid across the floor, CATCHING and REFRACTING LIGHT, I watch RAINDROPS scintillate a PUDDLE, STREAM down a windowpane, I disturb the surface of a sink full of WATER, watching RIPPLES propagate and INTERFERE, I BOUNCE a ball against a corner of my room, studying its trajectory . . .

Cut to:

EXT. INSTITUTE FOR ADVANCED STUDY, PRINCETON – DAY (B&W)

Strauss watches Oppenheimer hand the HAT *to Einstein. Strauss checks his watch, then starts down the hill towards them. As he approaches, Einstein* TURNS, *walking towards Strauss with a* GRIM EXPRESSION . . .

> STRAUSS
> (friendly)
>
> Albert . . .

Einstein PASSES *without acknowledging Strauss. Strauss reaches Oppenheimer –*

> STRAUSS
> What did you say to him?

> OPPENHEIMER
> He's fine. Mr Strauss, there are things in my past you need to be aware of.

> STRAUSS
> As Chairman of the AEC I have access to your security file. I've read it. The job's yours.

> OPPENHEIMER
> You're not worried?

> STRAUSS
> After all you've done for your country?

15

OPPENHEIMER
Times change, Mr Strauss.

STRAUSS
The purpose of this Institute is to provide a haven for independent minds. You're the man for the job.

OPPENHEIMER
Then I'll consider it. And I'll see you at the AEC meeting tomorrow.

Oppenheimer turns, heads back up the hill.

STRAUSS
(taken aback)
This is one of the most prestigious appointments in the country . . .

Oppenheimer looks back at Strauss, GRINS –

OPPENHEIMER
With a great commute. That's why I'm considering it.

Strauss watches him go, shaking his head.

SENATOR McGEE
(V.O.)
So, Dr Oppenheimer brought your attention to his past associations <u>before</u> *you appointed him?*

INT. SENATE COMMITTEE HEARING ROOM – DAY
(B & W)

STRAUSS
Yes.

SENATOR McGEE
And they didn't concern you?

STRAUSS
Just then I was more concerned about what he'd said to Einstein to sour him on me.

A few CHUCKLES *from the room.*

> SENATOR McGEE
> But later?

> STRAUSS
> *Well, we all know what happened later.*

Cut to:

INT. ROOM 2022, ATOMIC ENERGY COMMISSION –
DAY (COLOUR)

The board members listen as I continue reading . . .

> OPPENHEIMER
> After Gottingen I moved on to Leiden in Holland . . .

INT. LECTURE HALL, LEIDEN – DAY

A packed hall. The Young Me nervously checks my notes.

> OPPENHEIMER
> (V.O.)
> . . . where I first met Isidor Rabi . . .

A stocky young man, ISIDOR RABI (thirty), plonks down next to
a DUTCH STUDENT who reluctantly shifts, giving him room.

> RABI
> A Yank lecturing on the new physics? This I have to hear –
> I'm an American myself.

> DUTCH STUDENT
> How surprising.

> RABI
> Let me know if you need any help with the English.

I start lecturing . . . IN DUTCH. Rabi, confused, leans in.

> RABI
> Wait, what's he saying?

INT. TRAIN, LEIDEN TO ZURICH – NIGHT

I stare out the window at dark trees, steam and shadows. Rabi dumps his bags down, slumps opposite, sizes me up. Offers me an orange –

> YOUNG OPPENHEIMER
> No, thank you.

> RABI
> It's a long way to Zurich. You get any skinnier we might lose you between the seat cushions. I'm Rabi.

> YOUNG OPPENHEIMER
> Oppenheimer.

Rabi starts peeling his orange.

> RABI
> I caught your lecture on molecules. Caught *some* of it – we're a couple of New York Jews – how do you know Dutch?

> YOUNG OPPENHEIMER
> I thought I'd better learn it when I got here this semester.

Rabi STOPS peeling his orange to STARE at me –

> RABI
> You learned enough Dutch in *six weeks* to give a lecture on quantum mechanics?

> YOUNG OPPENHEIMER
> I wanted to challenge myself.

> RABI
> Quantum physics isn't challenging enough? Schvitzer.

> YOUNG OPPENHEIMER
> Shvitzer?

> RABI
> 'Show-off.' Dutch in six weeks but you never learned Yiddish?

> YOUNG OPPENHEIMER
> (smile)
> They don't speak it so much my side of the Park.

> RABI
> Screw you. Homesick?

> YOUNG OPPENHEIMER
> You know it.

Rabi peels his orange. He turns serious . . .

> RABI
> Ever get the feeling our kind isn't entirely welcome here?

> YOUNG OPPENHEIMER
> Physicists?

> RABI
> Funny.

> YOUNG OPPENHEIMER
> Sometimes. Not in the department.

> RABI
> They're all Jewish, too.

Rabi tosses me a slice of orange.

> RABI
> Eat.

I take the orange, 'sipping' at it.

> RABI
> In Zurich there's a German you *have* to seek out –

> YOUNG OPPENHEIMER
> Heisenberg.

INT. LECTURE HALL, ZURICH – DAY

A tall man of twenty-six turns from the blackboard –
HEISENBERG. I study his every move. Rabi NUDGES me 'See?' . . .

INT. SAME – LATER

Rabi introduces me to Heisenberg.

> HEISENBERG
> Oppenheimer, yes. I liked your paper on molecules.

> OPPENHEIMER
> Probably because you inspired it.

> HEISENBERG
> If I inspire anything else, let me know. We could publish together.

> OPPENHEIMER
> I have to get back to America.

> HEISENBERG
> Why? There's no one there taking quantum mechanics seriously.

> OPPENHEIMER
> That's *exactly* why.

> RABI
> He's pining for the canyons of Manhattan.

> OPPENHEIMER
> The canyons of New Mexico.

> HEISENBERG
> You're from New Mexico?

> OPPENHEIMER
> New York, but my brother and I have a ranch outside Santa Fe. That's the America I miss right now.

> HEISENBERG
> Then you best get home, cowboys.

> RABI
> That's *his* thing – me and horses? I don't think so.

GRAY
(V.O.)
Did you ever encounter Heisenberg again?

INT. ROOM 2022, ATOMIC ENERGY COMMISSION –
DAY

I smile to myself.

OPPENHEIMER
Not in person. But you might say our paths crossed.

ROBB
Doctor, during your time in Europe, you seem to have met
a wide range of other countries' physicists . . .
(consulting notes)
Born, Bohr, Pauli, Dirac, Einstein, Heisenberg . . . ?

OPPENHEIMER
That's right.

Robb looks up at me . . .

ROBB
Any Russians?

OPPENHEIMER
None that spring to mind.
(from notes)
Returning to America I accepted appointments at both
Caltech . . .

EXT. BERKELEY – DAY

I walk across campus to the physics department . . .

OPPENHEIMER
(V.O.)
. . . and up at Berkeley.

INT. CORRIDOR, BERKELEY – CONTINUOUS

I struggle to unlock a door . . . it opens –

INT. CLASSROOM, BERKELEY – CONTINUOUS

A DUSTY storage space. Scattered tables and chairs. A piano.

EXT. CORRIDOR, BERKELEY – MOMENTS LATER

I step out of the classroom. Look NEXT DOOR . . .

INT. RAD LAB, BERKELEY – DAY

I enter. A handsome young scientist, ERNEST LAWRENCE, works
on an assemblage of curved pipes and wiring with students,
including Luis ALVAREZ.

> OPPENHEIMER
> Dr Lawrence, I presume.

> LAWRENCE
> You must be Oppenheimer. I hear you want to start a
> school of quantum theory.

> OPPENHEIMER
> I *am* starting it. Next door.

> LAWRENCE
> They put you in there?

> OPPENHEIMER
> I asked for it. I wanted to be close to you experimentalists.

> LAWRENCE
> Theory will get you only so far.
> (gestures)
> We're building a machine to accelerate electrons.

> OPPENHEIMER
> Magnificent.

                    LAWRENCE
Would you like to help?

                    OPPENHEIMER
Build it? No. But I'm working on theories I'd like to test
with it.

                    LAWRENCE
When do you start teaching?

                    OPPENHEIMER
I've got my first in an hour.

                    LAWRENCE
Seminar?

                    OPPENHEIMER
Pupil.

                    LAWRENCE
One student? That's it?

                    OPPENHEIMER
I'm teaching something no one here's dreamt of. But once
people start hearing what you can do with it . . .

                    LAWRENCE
                    (grins)
There's no going back.

INT. CLASSROOM, BERKELEY – LATER

I stand there, expectant. A student opens the door, looks around,
embarrassed –

                    STUDENT
I'm sorry, I must have missed –

                    OPPENHEIMER
No, this is it. Mr Lomanitz, right?

LOMANITZ (twenty-one) nods, takes a seat.

OPPENHEIMER
What do you know about quantum mechanics?

LOMANITZ
I have a grasp on the basics –

OPPENHEIMER
Then you're doing it wrong.
(rapid-fire)
Is light made up of particles or waves?

Lomanitz opens his mouth to speak – too slow –

OPPENHEIMER
Quantum mechanics says it's both – how can it be both?

LOMANITZ
It can't.

OPPENHEIMER
It can't. But it is. It's paradoxical and yet . . . it *works*.

Lomanitz is hooked. I turn to the board, chalk out an
equation . . . when I turn back –

There are now FIVE students (including SERBER and SNYDER)
listening intently . . . I move to Lomanitz to hand him his paper.
I pat his shoulder.

OPPENHEIMER
You're gonna be okay.

Dissolve to:

A PACKED CLASSROOM, hanging on my every word as I – now
thirty-two, slim, well-dressed, confident – teach in the round.
Lawrence listens at the edge, fascinated.

OPPENHEIMER
Consider a star . . . a vast furnace burning in outer
space . . .

INSERT CUT: A STAR. A SUN. BURNING, ROILING.

OPPENHEIMER

Fire pushing outwards against its own gravity – balanced.
But if its furnace cools, gravity starts winning. It
contracts . . .

I look around. Make eye contact with Hartland SNYDER . . .

SNYDER

Density increases . . .

OPPENHEIMER

Increasing gravity . . .

INSERT CUT: THE SUN IS SHRINKING, MORE AND MORE
RAPIDLY . . .

SNYDER

Increasing density. A vicious cycle. Until . . . What's the
limit here?

OPPENHEIMER

I don't know. See where the math takes us. I guarantee it's
somewhere no one's been before.

SNYDER

Me?

OPPENHEIMER

Your math's better than mine.

EXT. BERKELEY – DAY

Energetic, dashing, I STRIDE across campus, a group of students,
including Snyder and Lomanitz, following me, hanging on my
every word . . .

OPPENHEIMER

Einstein can't accept the Copenhagen interpretation –

LOMANITZ

'God doesn't play dice.'

OPPENHEIMER
Except he does. Bohr showed us how . . .

INT. CLASSROOM, BERKELEY – DAY

I mark up a paper. Lawrence comes in, frowns at the board.

LAWRENCE
You shouldn't let them bring their politics into the
classroom . . .

I follow his look: 'SATURDAY 2:00pm, RALLY FOR
LOYALIST SPAIN'.

OPPENHEIMER
I wrote that. Lawrence, you embrace the revolution
in physics, can't you see it everywhere else? Picasso,
Stravinsky, Freud, Marx . . .

LAWRENCE
This is America, Oppie. We had our revolution. Seriously,
keep it out of the lab.

OPPENHEIMER
Well, *out of the lab*, my landlady's having a discussion
group tonight.

LAWRENCE
I've sampled the Berkeley political scene – it's all
philosophy postgrads and Communists talking integration.

OPPENHEIMER
You don't care about integration?

LAWRENCE
I want to vote for it, not talk about it. Let's get dinner.

OPPENHEIMER
I'm meeting my brother there.

SENATOR BARTLETT
(V.O.)
Dr Oppenheimer's file contained details of FBI surveillance on his activities at Berkeley . . .

INT. SENATE COMMITTEE HEARING ROOM – DAY
(B&W)

Strauss looks at the senator, cautious . . .

STRAUSS
Yes, as I recall.

SENATOR BARTLETT
Why would they have started a file on Dr Oppenheimer before the war?

STRAUSS
You'd have to ask Mr Hoover.

SENATOR BARTLETT
I'm asking you, Admiral Strauss.

STRAUSS
My assumption is that it was connected to his left-wing political activities.

SENATOR BARTLETT
How would these activities have come to the attention of the FBI?

STRAUSS
Well, if I remember correctly . . .

Cut to:

EXT. HOUSE PARTY, SHASTA ROAD, BERKELEY – NIGHT (COLOUR)

> STRAUSS
> (V.O.)
> The FBI was taking license plates outside suspected Communist gatherings and his name popped up.

As I get out of my car, I spot TWO MEN checking the license plates of cars on the street . . . I am GRABBED –

> FRANK
> (O.S.)
> Gotcha!

My younger brother FRANK (twenty-five) and his date, JACKIE.

INT. LIVING ROOM, HOUSE PARTY, SHASTA ROAD, BERKELEY – NIGHT

We ENTER the bustling room – I spot a beguiling young woman –

> VOICE
> (O.S.)
> Robert! Come meet Chevalier.

Mary WASHBURN grabs my tie and leads us to Haakon CHEVALIER.

> WASHBURN
> Dr Haakon Chevalier, Dr Robert Oppenheimer, and vice versa.

> OPPENHEIMER
> This is my little brother, Frank. Oh, and . . . uh . . .

> JACKIE
> Still Jackie.

> CHEVALIER
> Hello, Still Jackie.

OPPENHEIMER
Chevalier. You're in languages.

CHEVALIER
And your reputation precedes you.

OPPENHEIMER
I'm blushing – what've you heard?

CHEVALIER
You're teaching a radical new approach to physics that
I have no chance of understanding. But I hadn't heard you
were a Party member –

OPPENHEIMER
I'm not.

FRANK
Not yet.

JACKIE
Frank and I are thinking of joining –

OPPENHEIMER
(ignoring Jackie)
I support a range of causes.

Jackie, put out, leads Frank away.

CHEVALIER
The Spanish Civil War?

OPPENHEIMER
A democratic republic being overthrown by fascist thugs?
Who wouldn't?

CHEVALIER
Our government – they think socialism's a bigger threat
than fascism.

OPPENHEIMER
Not for long – look at what the Nazis are doing to the
Jews. I send funds to colleagues in Germany to emigrate.
I have to do something. My own work is so . . . abstract.

29

CHEVALIER
What're you working on?

OPPENHEIMER
What happens to stars when they die.

CHEVALIER
Do stars die?

OPPENHEIMER
If they do they'd cool, then collapse. And the bigger the
star, the more violent its demise. Their gravity gets so
concentrated . . .

INSERT CUT: THE SUN SHRINKS. THE LIGHT OF THE DISTANT
STARS BEHIND IS TUGGED TOWARDS THE DYING STAR, BENDING,
STRETCHING.

OPPENHEIMER
It swallows everything. Even light.

CHEVALIER
Good God. Can that really happen?

OPPENHEIMER
The math says it can. If we can get published, maybe
one day an astronomer finds one. But all I have is theory.
Which can't impact people's lives.

CHEVALIER
If you're sending money to Spain, do it through the
Communist Party – they can get it to the front lines.

The beguiling young woman is there with a tray of martinis.
This is Jean TATLOCK . . .

TATLOCK
Mary sent me with these. I'm Jean.

OPPENHEIMER
Robert.

CHEVALIER

Haakon Chevalier. The union meeting at Serber's last month?

Tatlock nods. I take a glass.

CHEVALIER

Robert here says he's not a Communist.

TATLOCK

Then he doesn't know enough about it.

OPPENHEIMER

I've read *Das Kapital*. All three volumes. Does that count?

CHEVALIER

That would make you better read than most Party members.

OPPENHEIMER

It's turgid stuff, but there's some thinking . . . 'Ownership is theft.'

TATLOCK

'Property', not 'Ownership'.

OPPENHEIMER

Sorry, I read it in the original German.

Chevalier laughs, delighted, as he leaves us alone.

TATLOCK

It's not about the book, it's about the ideas. You sound uncommitted.

OPPENHEIMER

I'm committed to thinking freely about how to improve our world. Why limit yourself to one dogma?

TATLOCK

You're a physicist – do you pick and choose rules? Or do you use the discipline to channel your energies into progress?

                    OPPENHEIMER
I like a little wiggle room. Do you always toe the party
line?

Tatlock considers this. Sizes me up.

                    TATLOCK
I like my wiggle room, too.

INT. BEDROOM – LATER

We are FUCKING. Hot, sweaty, a little brutal. Tatlock GIVES UP,
climbs off me –

                    OPPENHEIMER
Wait, wait –

I catch my breath, watching her STUDY my shelves.

                    TATLOCK
Unexpected.

                    OPPENHEIMER
What?

                    TATLOCK
For a physicist.

                    OPPENHEIMER
You've only got a shelf full of Freud?

                    TATLOCK
Actually my background's more –

                    OPPENHEIMER
Jungian.

                    TATLOCK
You know analysis.

                    OPPENHEIMER
When I was a postgrad at Cambridge I had some trouble.

She turns to me.

                    TATLOCK

I'll bite.

                    OPPENHEIMER

I tried to poison my tutor.

                    TATLOCK

Did you hate him?

                    OPPENHEIMER

I liked him very much.

Tatlock turns back to the books.

                    TATLOCK

You just needed to get laid.

                    OPPENHEIMER

Wow. Took my analysts two years, and I'm not sure they
ever put it that succinctly.

                    TATLOCK

You had them convinced you're more complicated than
you really are.

                    OPPENHEIMER

We're all simple souls, I guess.

                    TATLOCK

Not me.

She pulls a book from the shelf: THE BHAGAVAD GITA. She opens
the book to find INCOMPREHENSIBLE CHARACTERS.

                    TATLOCK

What's this?

                    OPPENHEIMER

Sanskrit.

                    TATLOCK

You can read this?

                    OPPENHEIMER

I'm learning –

She climbs on top of me, opens the book in my face.

> TATLOCK
> Go on, then.

I study the page as Tatlock starts to move.

> OPPENHEIMER
> In this part, Vishnu reveals his multi-armed self –

> TATLOCK
> Read the words.

She points to each word as I translate . . .

> OPPENHEIMER
> 'And now I am become Death . . .

She nods, impressed, starts moving again . . .

> OPPENHEIMER
> . . . destroyer of worlds.'

EXT. NEW MEXICO – DAY

Moving over the VAST landscape to find three tiny figures. I lead Lawrence and Frank on horseback up a mountain trail.

EXT. CAMPSITE – EVENING

THUNDER. Lawrence climbs off his horse. The wind WHIPS as we set up our tent . . .

> OPPENHEIMER
> It'll break before dawn. The air cools overnight. Just before dawn, the storm dies.

INT./EXT. TENT – NIGHT

Lawrence, Frank and I huddle in the BUFFETING TENT, trying to keep a fire going in the WIND and RAIN outside the tent.

                            FRANK
  I'm getting married.

                          LAWRENCE
  Congratulations, Frank.

I look at Frank, sardonic with drink.

                        OPPENHEIMER
  To Jackie?

Frank stares at me . . . the tent stops buffeting . . .

                            FRANK
  Yeah, to Jackie. The waitress.

                          LAWRENCE
                      (sensing tension)
  Oppie, you're right – it's letting up. I'll see if there's any
  stars.

Frank watches Lawrence go, then pounces –

                            FRANK
  All your talk about the common man but Jackie's not
  good enough? We join the Party – you can't hide your
  disapproval – why? Because that's supposed to be *your*
  thing –?

                        OPPENHEIMER
  I haven't joined the Party, Frank. And I don't think she
  should've convinced you to, either –

                            FRANK
  Half the faculty's Communist –

                        OPPENHEIMER
  Not that half.

I point in the direction Lawrence wandered off.

                        OPPENHEIMER
  I'm your brother, and I want you to be cautious.

                              35

FRANK

And I want to wring your neck.

I giggle at this. Frank shakes his head, then starts laughing, too. I grab Frank's shoulder. Frank looks up . . .

FRANK

Robert, I won't live my life afraid to make a mistake.

I hold up my hands in defeat –

OPPENHEIMER

You're happy, I'm happy.

FRANK

Then I'm happy you're happy.

EXT. PERRO CALIENTE – MOMENTS LATER

I approach Lawrence, who stares up at the stars.

LAWRENCE

It's so clear I feel like I could see one of those dark stars you're working on . . .

OPPENHEIMER

You can't, that's the whole point.

INSERT CUT: AN EXPANDING DARKNESS EATS THE STARS . . .

OPPENHEIMER

Their gravity swallows light. It's like a kind of . . . hole in space.

LAWRENCE

Is Frank okay?

OPPENHEIMER

Yeah. He just has a shitty brother.

Lawrence smiles at this. Looks around them.

LAWRENCE

It's special here.

OPPENHEIMER

As a kid I thought if I could find a way to combine physics and New Mexico, my life would be perfect.

LAWRENCE

It's a little remote for that.

OPPENHEIMER

Let's get some sleep.

I turn, heading to the tent. Lawrence follows.

OPPENHEIMER

That mesa we saw today? One of my favorite places in the world. Tomorrow we'll climb it.

LAWRENCE

What's it called?

My response is so soft it is almost swallowed by the dark . . .

OPPENHEIMER

Los Alamos.

EXT. STREET, BERKELEY – DAY

Tatlock and I walk down the sidewalk. I try to take her hand – she folds her arms.

TATLOCK

I wasn't expecting to see you.

OPPENHEIMER

I have to make an appointment?

Across the street a young man BURSTS out of the BARBER SHOP, towel across chest, NEWSPAPER in hand . . . the barber runs out – the young man rips off the towel, TOSSES it to him and RUNS –

OPPENHEIMER

Alvarez!

I leave Tatlock on the sidewalk, take off after Alverez –

37

EXT. BERKELEY CAMPUS – DAY

Alvarez SPRINTS, newspaper in hand – I follow –

INT. CLASSROOM, BERKELEY – CONTINUOUS

I BURST in – Lawrence is trying to calm Alvarez –

> ALVAREZ
> (breathless)
> They've done it! Hahn and Strassman in Germany . . .

Alvarez tosses the paper at me –

> ALVAREZ
> They split the uranium nucleus.

> LAWRENCE
> How?

> OPPENHEIMER
> (reading)
> Bombarded it with neutrons.

> ALVAREZ
> Lawrence, it's fission. *Nuclear* fission. They've split the atom . . .

> OPPENHEIMER
> It's not possible.

I put down the paper, take up my chalk like it's a weapon, move to the board. Alvarez grabs the paper –

> ALVAREZ
> I'm going to try to reproduce it.

Alvarez and Lawrence leave. I write and write . . .

INT. CLASSROOM, BERKELEY – LATER

Lawrence enters. I turn. Point at the board.

                    OPPENHEIMER
See. It can't be done.

                    LAWRENCE
Very elegant. Quite clear. Just one problem . . .

                    OPPENHEIMER
Where?

                    LAWRENCE
Next door. Alvarez did it.

INT. RAD LAB, BERKELEY – MOMENTS LATER

I peer at Alvarez's oscilloscope . . .

                    LAWRENCE
Theory will take you only so far.

I stand, moving away . . . thinking . . .

                    OPPENHEIMER
During the process extra neutrons boil off. Which could be
used to split other uranium atoms . . .

                    LAWRENCE
A chain reaction. You're thinking what I'm thinking.

                    OPPENHEIMER
You, me and every physicist around the world who's seen
the news.

                    ALVAREZ
What? What're we all thinking?

                    OPPENHEIMER
A bomb, Alvarez. A bomb.

EXT. TATLOCK HOUSE, BERKELEY – NIGHT

Tatlock GRABS a bouquet out of my hands –

                    TATLOCK
I told you, Robert, no more fucking flowers.

39

She dumps them in the trash. I just stare.

> OPPENHEIMER
> I don't understand what you want from me –

> TATLOCK
> I don't want *anything* from you.

I pause. Then, gently . . .

> OPPENHEIMER
> You say that. Then you call.

Tatlock kicks at the dirt.

> TATLOCK
> Don't answer.

> OPPENHEIMER
> I'll always answer.

She looks up at me.

> TATLOCK
> Fine. But no more flowers.

She goes inside –

> OPPENHEIMER
> Aren't you coming?

Slams the door shut behind her. I stand there.

> CHEVALIER
> (O.S.)
> You have to know when you're beaten, Robert.

I turn. Chevalier and his wife, BARBARA, wait in the car.

> OPPENHEIMER
> It's not that simple, Haakon.

INT. MEETING HALL, BERKELEY – NIGHT

Chevalier and Barbara lead me into the crowded hall. A
BANNER – 'FEDERATION OF ARCHITECTS, ENGINEERS,
CHEMISTS AND TECHNICIANS'.

A man with a British accent greets us. This is ELTENTON.

> ELTENTON
> Chevalier, good to see you. And the illustrious
> Dr Oppenheimer. I'm Eltenton. Might you say a word
> about organized labour on campuses?

> OPPENHEIMER
> I'll try to think of something.

Eltenton guides me towards the stage . . .

> ELTENTON
> I work at Shell, we've signed up chemists *and* engineers . . .

> OPPENHEIMER
> That's excellent.

I spot Lomanitz, who grins and waves . . .

> ELTENTON
> So why not scientists in academia?

> OPPENHEIMER
> Sure. When do we –

Eltenton pushes me onto the stage. People start APPLAUDING at
the very sight of me. I can't quite not smile about this.

INT. RAD LAB, BERKELEY – DAY

I watch Lawrence examine his cyclotron.

> OPPENHEIMER
> Teachers are unionized, Lawrence. Why not professors?

> LAWRENCE
> Don't you have somewhere to be?

41

OPPENHEIMER
Academics have rights, too –

LAWRENCE
It's not that. I have a group coming.

OPPENHEIMER
I'll sit in.

LAWRENCE
Not this one.

The door opens. Richard TOLMAN and Vannevar BUSH enter –

OPPENHEIMER
Richard. Dr Bush. What brings you two up north?

They exchange glances with Lawrence. Awkward SILENCE. I rise, letting them off the hook –

OPPENHEIMER
Richard, tell Ruth I'll be down to Pasadena Thursday.

INT. CLASSROOM, BERKELEY – CONTINUOUS

As I enter, a magazine FLAPS into my hands from across the room. Students are all reading copies . . .

SERBER
Your paper on black holes – it's in!

I open the magazine as I turn to a STUDENT –

OPPENHEIMER
Get Hartland.

LOMANITZ
September 1st, 1939 – the world's gonna remember this day . . .

Snyder comes in with a newspaper. Glum.

OPPENHEIMER
Hartland, our paper, it's in print!

SNYDER

We've been upstaged.

He holds up the paper: 'HITLER INVADES POLAND'.

OPPENHEIMER
(V.O.)
During the Battle of France and the Battle of Britain . . .

INT. ROOM 2022, ATOMIC ENERGY COMMISSION –
DAY

Robb looks on intently as I turn the page on my statement . . .

OPPENHEIMER
. . . I found myself increasingly out of sympathy with the
policy of neutrality that Communists advocated.

ROBB
And after Hitler invaded Russia, did these Communist
sympathies return?

OPPENHEIMER
No. If you'll just allow me to –

GRAY
Mr Robb, you'll have ample opportunity to cross-examine.

OPPENHEIMER
I need to make clear that my changing opinion of Russia
did not mean a sharp break with those who held different
views. For a year or two during a previous marriage my
wife, Kitty, had been a Communist Party member.

Behind me, on a couch, is KITTY (forty-six), listening intently . . .

OPPENHEIMER
But when I first met her, in Pasadena in 1939, she had
already disengaged from politics . . .

INT. HOUSE PARTY, TOLMAN HOUSE, PASADENA —
NIGHT

Kitty (thirty-one) watches as I EXPERTLY open the liquor
cabinet –

> OPPENHEIMER
> This is where I keep the good stuff.

> KITTY
> I thought this was the Tolmans' house.

> OPPENHEIMER
> I live with them when I'm at Caltech.

> RUTH
> (O.S.)
> You two need anything?

I turn to see RUTH TOLMAN (forty-five) looking at me,
mischievous.

> OPPENHEIMER
> We're fine, Ruthie.
> (to Kitty)
> You're a biologist?

> KITTY
> Somehow I graduated to housewife. Can you explain
> quantum mechanics to me? It seems baffling.

> OPPENHEIMER
> It is. This glass –

I thump a glass onto the cabinet – pour a drink –

> OPPENHEIMER
> This drink –

I hand her the glass – fingers touching . . .

> OPPENHEIMER
> Our bodies . . . are mostly empty space – groupings of tiny
> energy waves bound together.

                                KITTY
By what?

                             OPPENHEIMER
Forces of attraction strong enough to convince us that
matter is solid . . .

I push the palm of my hand up against hers.

                             OPPENHEIMER
And stop my body passing through yours.

Kitty pushes her fingers through mine, interlacing our hands.
I look at a GREY-HAIRED MAN in conversation with Tolman . . .

                             OPPENHEIMER
You're married to Dr Harrison.

                                KITTY
Not very.

                             OPPENHEIMER
Well, there's someone that I . . .

                                KITTY
Does she feel the same way?

                             OPPENHEIMER
Sometimes. Not often enough.

As Ruth looks our way I let Kitty's hand go.

                             OPPENHEIMER
I'm going to New Mexico, to my ranch. With friends. You
should come.

Kitty looks meaningfully over her glass at me.

                             OPPENHEIMER
I meant with your husband.

                                KITTY
Yes, you did. Because you know it won't make a bit of
difference.

EXT. PERRO CALIENTE — DAY

Kitty and I THUNDER along on horseback, climbing a ridge.
I shout ahead to Kitty –

                    OPPENHEIMER
        Why did you marry him?!

Kitty pulls up. I come alongside.

                    KITTY
        I was lost. He was kind.

                    OPPENHEIMER
        Lost?

                    KITTY
        My previous husband died. At twenty-eight I wasn't ready
        to be a widow.

Kitty DISMOUNTS. I follow.

                    OPPENHEIMER
        Who was your first husband?

                    KITTY
        Nobody. But my *second* husband was Joe Dallet.
        From money, like me, but he was a union organizer in
        Youngstown, Ohio. I fell hard.

                    OPPENHEIMER
        How hard?

                    KITTY
        Hard enough to spend four years living off beans and
        pancakes, handing out the *Daily Worker* at factory gates.

Kitty takes out a hip flask. SWIGS.

                    KITTY
        By '36 I told Joe I couldn't take it anymore, quit the Party
        and joined my parents swanning around Europe. A year
        later I said I wanted him back. Him, not the *Daily Worker*.
        He said 'Swell, I'll meet you on my way to Spain.'

She hands me the flask. I take a drink.

> OPPENHEIMER
> He went to fight for the loyalists?

> KITTY
> On his way we reconciled. One beautiful week in Paris.
> Then he went to the brigades and I waited. One day Steve
> Nelson turns up in the lobby of the hotel to tell me Joe got
> himself killed first time he popped out of his trench.

> OPPENHEIMER
> Who's Steve Nelson?

> KITTY
> Head of the Communist Party in San Francisco. You don't
> know him?

> OPPENHEIMER
> I'm not a Communist.

> KITTY
> You seem to know a lot of 'em.

> OPPENHEIMER
> Including you.

> KITTY
> (shakes head)
> Ideology got Joe killed. For nothing.

> OPPENHEIMER
> The Spanish Republic isn't nothing.

> KITTY
> My husband offered both our futures to stop one fascist
> bullet embedding itself in a mudbank. That's the *definition*
> of nothing.

> OPPENHEIMER
> That seems a little reductive –

                              KITTY
Pragmatic. Steve and his wife brought me home with them
to Chicago, then set me up with husband number three.
Now here I am . . .

She looks around at the wilderness . . .

                              KITTY
Wherever the *hell* this is –

I grab her. Kiss her, hard.

INT. TATLOCK'S BEDROOM – DAY

Tatlock and I sit on the floor, backs to the bed like kids. Tatlock
has been crying.

                         OPPENHEIMER
I didn't want you to hear it from someone else.

                            TATLOCK
You didn't bring flowers. That's something.

I reach into my pocket – she GRABS the small posy from me,
TOSSING it aside.

                         OPPENHEIMER
Jean, we both know I'm not what you want.

                            TATLOCK
Yeah. But it's a door closing.

                         OPPENHEIMER
Not as far as I'm concerned.

Tatlock looks at me. Appreciating the sentiment.

                            TATLOCK
You knocked her up. Fast work.

                         OPPENHEIMER
Can't keep a good man down.

TATLOCK

I meant *her*. She knew what she wanted. What about the husband?

OPPENHEIMER

We spoke. He's divorcing her so we can get married before she's showing.

TATLOCK

How civilized, you idiot. This is your community – you think rules don't apply to the golden boy?

OPPENHEIMER

Brilliance makes up for a lot.

TATLOCK

Don't alienate the only people in the world who understand what you do. One day you might need them.

INT. RAD LAB, BERKELEY – DAY

I write 'F.A.E.C.T.' on the board, Lomanitz hands out FLIERS. Lawrence enters, GRABBING a flyer from the nearest student – 'UNIONIZE THE RADIATION LAB'.

LAWRENCE

Lomanitz? What do you make a month?

LOMANITZ
(sheepish)
A hundred and fifty dollars.

Lawrence turns to another student –

LAWRENCE

How are the working conditions?

OPPENHEIMER

That's not the point, Lawrence.

LAWRENCE

What do you have in common with dock workers and farm labourers?

49

LOMANITZ

Plenty –

LAWRENCE

Right. Everybody out. Now!
                    (to me)
Not you.

The students file out. Lawrence SLAMS the door – turns on me –

LAWRENCE

What're you doing?!

OPPENHEIMER

It's a trade union –

LAWRENCE

Full of Communists!

OPPENHEIMER

So? I haven't joined the Party –

LAWRENCE

They won't let me bring you onto the project because of this shit! They won't even let me tell you what the project *is* –

OPPENHEIMER

I know what the fucking project is, Lawrence! We all heard about Einstein and Szilard's letter to Roosevelt. Warning him the Germans could make a bomb. And *I* know what it means for the Nazis to have a bomb.

LAWRENCE

I don't?

OPPENHEIMER

It's not your people they're herding into camps! It's mine!

LAWRENCE

You think *I* tell them about your politics? Next time you're coming home from a meeting, take a look in the rear-view mirror. Listen for sounds on your phone line. And stop being so goddamn naive.

I'm taken aback by this . . .

> OPPENHEIMER
> Why would they care what I do?

> LAWRENCE
> Because you're not just self-important, you're *actually* important.

I see the reality. Shift gears –

> OPPENHEIMER
> I get it. You don't have to worry. I get it.

> LAWRENCE
> You just need to be more –

> OPPENHEIMER
> Pragmatic. It's done, Lawrence. I'll talk to Lomanitz and the others. You don't have to worry.

Lawrence looks at me. Sees this is real.

> LAWRENCE
> Then welcome to the war.

> OPPENHEIMER
> (V.O.)
> I filled out my first security questionnaire . . .

INT. ROOM 2022, ATOMIC ENERGY COMMISSION – DAY

I glance up from my notes.

> OPPENHEIMER
> . . . and was informed that my involvement in left-wing groups would not prove a bar to my work on the atomic programme.

SENATOR PASTORE
(V.O.)
Why were his Communist associations not seen as a
security risk during the war?

Cut to:

INT. SENATE COMMITTEE HEARING ROOM – DAY
(B&W)

Strauss suppresses his irritation at the line of questioning.

STRAUSS
*Senator, I can't possibly answer for a security clearance
granted years before I even met the man.*

SENATOR PASTORE
Fine. What about after?

STRAUSS
*After the war, Dr Oppenheimer was the most respected
scientific voice in the world. That's why I asked him to
run the Institute, that's why he advised the Atomic Energy
Commission. Simple as that.*

INT. SENATE OFFICE – DAY (B&W)

Strauss paces –

STRAUSS
What are they accusing me of?

SENATE AIDE
*I think they just want to know what happened between
1947 and 1954 to change your mind on Oppenheimer's
security clearance.*

STRAUSS
*I didn't. I was the AEC Chairman, but it wasn't me who
brought the charges against Robert.*

SENATE AIDE

Who did?

STRAUSS

*Some former staff member of the Joint Congressional
Committee –*

INSERT CUT: A YOUNG MAN LEAFS THROUGH A FILE, COLLECTING
HIS THOUGHTS . . . THIS IS WILLIAM BORDEN . . . HE STARTS
TYPING . . .

STRAUSS

*A rabid anti-Communist named Borden. He wrote to the
FBI demanding they take action.*

SENATE AIDE

The FBI? Why not come to the AEC direct?

STRAUSS

Why get caught holding the knife yourself?

SENATE AIDE

What did Borden have against Oppenheimer?

STRAUSS

*This was the McCarthy era – people hounded out of jobs
for any hint of red . . . reading Oppenheimer's security
file – his Communist brother, sister-in-law, fiancée, best
friend, wife . . . that's before you even get to the Chevalier
incident.*

SENATE AIDE

*But how would Borden have access to Oppenheimer's
security file?*

STRAUSS

*Someone gave it to him. Someone who wanted
Oppenheimer silenced.*

SENATE AIDE

Who?

STRAUSS

Who knows? Robert didn't take care not to upset the power brokers in Washington. His opinions on the atom became definitive and he wasn't always patient with us mere mortals. I came in for plenty of harsh treatment. There was an AEC vote on the export of isotopes to Norway . . .

INT. CONGRESSIONAL HEARING ROOM – DAY (B&W)

Oppenheimer sits at the witness table with Joe VOLPE, *the AEC lawyer. Strauss is in the audience.*

STRAUSS
(V.O.)
They drafted in Robert to make me look a fool . . .

CONGRESSMAN
But, Dr Oppenheimer, one member of the AEC board thinks these isotopes could be useful to our enemies in the production of atomic weapons.

OPPENHEIMER
Congressman, you could use a shovel in making atomic weapons, in fact, you do. You could use a bottle of beer in making atomic weapons. In fact, you do.

LAUGHTER. *Strauss squirms, embarrassed.*

OPPENHEIMER
Isotopes aren't as useful as electronic components, but more useful than a sandwich. I'd put them somewhere in between.

Volpe looks at Strauss, who SMILES, GOOD-HUMOURED . . .

STRAUSS
(V.O.)
Genius is no guarantee of wisdom. How could this man who saw so much be so blind?

Cut to:

INT. OPPENHEIMER HOUSE, BERKELEY – NIGHT
(COLOUR)

I come in. The lights are off. A BABY'S CRIES echo . . .

OPPENHEIMER
Kitty?

She is in the dining room, in the dark, drink in hand.

OPPENHEIMER
Kitty, the project – I'm in.

She sips. SLIDES her drink down the table at me –

KITTY
Let's celebrate.

As the baby CRIES, Kitty comes to me, pulling at my clothes –

OPPENHEIMER
Don't you need to go to him?

KITTY
I've been going to him all fucking day . . .

She moves to kiss my neck – I look upstairs – she PUSHES me
away – GRABS her drink . . .

EXT./INT. CHEVALIER HOUSE – NIGHT

I carry the crying infant, PETER, to the front door. Knock.
Barbara opens it – sees my distraught face and takes Peter.

INT. LIVING ROOM, CHEVALIER HOUSE – MOMENTS
LATER

Chevalier hands me a drink. I stare into the liquid.

OPPENHEIMER
I'm ashamed to ask.

CHEVALIER
Anything.

OPPENHEIMER

Take Peter.

CHEVALIER

Sure.

OPPENHEIMER

No, for a while, Hoke. A *while*.

CHEVALIER

Does Kitty know you're here?

OPPENHEIMER
(I laugh)

Of course she fucking knows! We're awful. Selfish, awful
people . . .
(I down drink)

Forget I asked –

Chevalier puts out a hand to stop me rising . . .

CHEVALIER

Robert, you see *beyond* the world we live in. There's a
price to be paid for that. Of course we'll help.

EXT. NEW MEXICO – EVENING

Kitty and I GALLOP through the trees, EMERGING into the
twilight overlooking a valley. Kitty turns to the wind.

KITTY

Everything's changing, Robert.

OPPENHEIMER

Having a child was always –

KITTY
(impatient)

The world is pivoting in some new direction . . .
reforming . . . this is your moment.

OPPENHEIMER

We're putting together a group to study feasibility –

                              KITTY
'We' shouldn't be doing anything. *You* should. Lawrence
won't get this done. Or Tolman, or Rabi. *You* will.

INT. PRESIDENT'S DINING HALL, BERKELEY – DAY

A crowded and lavish lunch. I notice a large man in ARMY
UNIFORM, Colonel GROVES, sitting next to another soldier
(NICHOLS) with Bush and Tolman. I sidle up to Lawrence at the
buffet.

                         OPPENHEIMER
    Who's the uniform?

The husky GROVES spills sauce on his tunic, wipes at it.

                           LAWRENCE
    I thought you might know.

INT. CLASSROOM, BERKELEY – AFTERNOON

I am working. Groves and Lieutenant Colonel NICHOLS enter.

                            GROVES
    Dr Oppenheimer. I'm Colonel Groves, this is Lieutenant
    Colonel Nichols.

Groves pulls off his uniform jacket, TOSSES it to Nichols.

                            GROVES
    Get that dry-cleaned.

I watch Nichols leave.

                         OPPENHEIMER
    If that's how you treat a lieutenant colonel, I'd hate to see
    how you treat a humble physicist.

                            GROVES
    If I ever meet one I'll let you know.

                         OPPENHEIMER
    Ouch.

                              57

GROVES

Theatres of combat all over the world – but I have to stay in Washington.

OPPENHEIMER

Why?

GROVES

I built the Pentagon. The brass likes it so much they made me take over the Manhattan Engineer District.

OPPENHEIMER

Which is?

GROVES

Don't be a smart-ass. You know damn well what it is – you and half of every physics department across America. That's problem number one.

OPPENHEIMER

I thought problem number one would be securing enough uranium ore.

GROVES

Twelve hundred tons. Bought the day I took charge.

OPPENHEIMER

Processing?

GROVES

Just broke ground at Oak Ridge, Tennessee. Now I'm looking for a project director.

OPPENHEIMER

And my name came up.

GROVES

Nope. Even though you brought quantum physics to America. That made me curious.

OPPENHEIMER

What have you found out?

GROVES

You're a dilettante, womanizer, suspected Communist –

OPPENHEIMER

I'm a New Deal Democrat –

GROVES

I said 'suspected'. Unstable, theatrical, egotistical, neurotic.

OPPENHEIMER

Nothing good? Not even 'he's brilliant, but' . . .?

GROVES

Brilliance is taken for granted in your circles. So, no.
Only one person said anything good – Richard Tolman.
He thinks you've got integrity. But Tolman strikes me as
someone who knows science better than people.

OPPENHEIMER

Yet here you are. You don't take much on trust.

GROVES

I don't take anything on trust. Why don't you have a
Nobel Prize?

OPPENHEIMER

Why aren't you a general?

GROVES

They're making me one for this.

OPPENHEIMER

Maybe I'll have the same luck.

GROVES

A Nobel Prize for making a bomb?

OPPENHEIMER

Alfred Nobel invented dynamite.

GROVES

So how would you proceed?

OPPENHEIMER

You're talking about turning theory into a practical
weapons system faster than the Nazis.

GROVES

Who have a twelve-month head start.

OPPENHEIMER

Eighteen.

GROVES

How could you possibly know that?

OPPENHEIMER

Our fast neutron research took six months – the man
they've undoubtedly put in charge will have made that leap
instantly.

GROVES

Who do you think they put in charge?

OPPENHEIMER

Werner Heisenberg. He has the most intuitive
understanding of atomic structure I've ever seen.

GROVES

You know his work?

OPPENHEIMER

I know *him*. Just like I know Walther Bothe. Von
Weizsäcker. Diebner. In a straight race, the Germans win.
We've got one hope.

GROVES

Which is?

OPPENHEIMER

Anti-Semitism.

GROVES

What?

OPPENHEIMER

Hitler called quantum physics 'Jewish science'. Said it right to Einstein's face. Our one hope is that Hitler's so blinded by hate he's denied Heisenberg proper resources. Because it'll take *vast* resources. Our nation's best scientists, working together – right now they're scattered.

GROVES

Which gives us compartmentalization.

OPPENHEIMER

All minds have to see the whole task to contribute efficiently. Poor security *may* cost us the race, inefficiency *will*. The Germans know more than us, anyway.

GROVES

The Russians don't.

OPPENHEIMER

Remind me – who are we at war with?

GROVES

Someone with your past doesn't want to be seen downplaying the importance of security from our Communist allies.

OPPENHEIMER

Point taken. But no.

GROVES

You don't get to say 'no' to me –

OPPENHEIMER

It's my job to say 'no' to you when you're wrong –

GROVES

So you've got the job, now?

OPPENHEIMER

I'm considering it.

GROVES

I'm starting to see how you got your reputation. My
favorite response? 'Oppenheimer couldn't run a hamburger
stand.'

OPPENHEIMER

I couldn't. But I can run the Manhattan Project.

I turn to the blackboard. Take up my chalk.

OPPENHEIMER

There's a way to balance these things . . .
                    (I draw)
Leave the Rad Lab here at Berkeley under Lawrence,
Met Lab in Chicago under Szilard, large-scale refining –
where'd you say? Tennessee . . . all America's industrial
might and scientific innovation, connected by rail . . .
focused on one goal, one point in space and time, coming
together . . . *here*.

I have drawn a cross at the centre of the diagram.

GROVES

And where's that?

INSERT CUT: A BARBED-WIRE FENCE IS STRUNG OUT . . .

OPPENHEIMER

A secret labouratory. In the middle of nowhere. Self-
sufficient. Secure. Equipment, housing, the works. We keep
everyone there till it's done.

INSERT CUT: A SCHOOLHOUSE IS ERECTED. A CHURCH. A
STORE . . .

OPPENHEIMER
(V.O.)
It'll need a school, stores, a church . . .

INT. TRAIN, BERKELEY TO WASHINGTON, DC – DAY

I talk to Groves as Nichols looks on . . .

                    GROVES
Why?

                    OPPENHEIMER
If we don't let scientists bring their families, we'll never get
the best. You want security? Build a town, and build it fast.

                    GROVES
Where?

EXT. CAR, LOS ALAMOS – CONTINUOUS

Groves emerges, squinting into the brightness, taking in the
stark beauty. I greet him, arms spread wide.

                    OPPENHEIMER
Welcome to Los Alamos. There's a boys' school we'll have
to commandeer, and the local Indians come up here for
burial rites. Other than that, nothing for forty miles any
direction. And south-east, hundreds of miles of desert.
Enough to find the perfect spot.

                    GROVES
For?

                    OPPENHEIMER
Success.

Groves scans the horizon. Sniffs the air . . . turns to Nichols.

                    GROVES
Build him a town. Fast.
                    (to Oppenheimer)
Let's go recruit some scientists.

INT. TRAIN, SANTA FE TO BOSTON – NIGHT

I watch Groves go over a file.

                    OPPENHEIMER
How much can I tell them?

GROVES
(without looking up)
As much as you like, till you feel my boot on your balls.

INT. LECTURE HALL, HARVARD – DAY

Groves and I sit talking to BAINBRIDGE and DONALD.

BAINBRIDGE
I'm not a soldier, Oppie.

OPPENHEIMER
Soldier? He's a general –
(jab my thumb at Groves)
I got all the soldier I need. Maybe too much. I'm here
because you know isotopes, and you –
(to Donald)
know explosives better than anyone.

DONALD
But you can't tell us what you're doing?

I glance at Groves. Then CROSS my legs.

OPPENHEIMER
It's about unleashing the strong force before the Nazis do.

BAINBRIDGE
Oh my God.

INT. CORRIDOR, MIT – DAY

Groves and I walk with CONDON.

CONDON
Why? Why would I leave my family?

OPPENHEIMER
I told you, bring your family.

64

CONDON

Why would we go to the middle of nowhere for who knows how long?

OPPENHEIMER

A year or two. Or three.

CONDON

Why would you think I'd do that?

Groves SNAPS like a bulldog –

GROVES

Why? Why? How about because this is the most important fucking thing that's ever happened in the history of the world? How about that?

I look at Groves, then SHRUG at Condon.

INT. OFFICE, UNIVERSITY OF MICHIGAN – NIGHT

Groves and I sit across the desk from a CONCERNED SCIENTIST.

CONCERNED SCIENTIST

Robert, I hear you. I hear you.

Concerned Scientist GLANCES at Groves then DROPS his gaze.

OPPENHEIMER

General, could you give us a minute?

Groves looks at me. Gets up and goes.

CONCERNED SCIENTIST

They're not gonna let someone like me onto this project. And failing a security check isn't gonna be good for a career even after the war.

OPPENHEIMER

So you're a fellow traveler, so what? This is a national emergency. I've got some skeletons, and they've put me in charge. They need us.

CONCERNED SCIENTIST
Until they don't.

INT. QUADRANGLE, PRINCETON – DAY

Groves and I flank FEYNMAN as he hurries across the quad –

OPPENHEIMER
Heisenberg, Diebner, Bothe, Bohr . . . what do these men
have in common?

FEYNMAN
The greatest minds on atomic theory.

OPPENHEIMER
And?

FEYNMAN
I don't know . . .

OPPENHEIMER
The Nazis have them.

FEYNMAN
Niels Bohr is in Copenhagen.

OPPENHEIMER
Under Nazi occupation. Did they stop printing newspapers
in Princeton?

FEYNMAN
Niels won't work for the Nazis.

OPPENHEIMER
No. Never. But while *they* have him, *we* don't. So I need
you.

INT. TRAIN, PRINCETON TO SANTA FE – NIGHT

Groves is napping. I just start talking.

OPPENHEIMER
Is there any chance of getting Bohr out of Denmark?

GROVES

No dice. I checked with the British. Until we get Allied boots back onto the continent there's no way. Is he that important?

INSERT CUT: BOHR GESTICULATES WITH THE POISONED APPLE.

OPPENHEIMER

How many people do you know who've proven Einstein wrong?

The train BUMPS. I look out the window, impatient.

OPPENHEIMER

It'd be quicker to take a plane.

GROVES

We can't risk a plane. America needs us.

EXT. LOS ALAMOS UNDER CONSTRUCTION – DAY

Dressed in ARMY UNIFORM, I show Rabi and Condon the CHAOTIC SNOWY and MUDDY mesa. CONSTRUCTION CREWS at work. Feynman approaches –

FEYNMAN

The Harvard guys say the building's too small for their cyclotron.

OPPENHEIMER
(to Condon)

Get 'em together with the architects.

Condon hurries off with Feynman. Rabi turns to me.

RABI

When's this place supposed to open?

OPPENHEIMER

Two months.

                          RABI
                     (shakes head)
Robert, you're the great improvizer, but *this* you can't do
in your head . . .

INT. CONSTRUCTION CABIN, LOS ALAMOS – MOMENTS
LATER

I draw on the board.

                        OPPENHEIMER
Four divisions – Experimental, Theoretical, Metallurgical,
Ordnance.

                          RABI
Who's running Theoretical?

                        OPPENHEIMER
I am.

                          RABI
That's what I was afraid of. You're spread too thin.

                        OPPENHEIMER
So *you* take Theoretical.

                          RABI
I'm not coming here, Robert.

                        OPPENHEIMER
Why not?

Rabi, seldom at a loss for words, is lost for words . . .

                          RABI
You drop a bomb and it falls on the just and the unjust.
I don't wish the culmination of three centuries of physics
to be a weapon of mass destruction.

                        OPPENHEIMER
Izzy, I don't know if we can be trusted with such a weapon,
but I know the Nazis can't. We have no choice.

RABI

Well, the second thing you have to do is appoint Hans
Bethe to head the Theoretical division.

OPPENHEIMER

Wait, what was the first?

RABI

Take off that ridiculous uniform – you're a scientist.

OPPENHEIMER

General Groves is insisting we join.

RABI

Tell Groves to shit in his hat. They need us for who we are.
So be yourself, only . . . better.

INT. OPPENHEIMER'S OFFICE, LOS ALAMOS – DAY

I pull on a jacket. Run a hand through newly shorn close-
cropped dark hair. Put on a PORK PIE HAT. Pick up my pipe . . .

EXT. LOS ALAMOS UNDER CONSTRUCTION – MOMENTS
LATER

I walk the main drag like a SHERIFF, nodding at construction
workers as I pass . . . THE ICONIC J. ROBERT OPPENHEIMER.

INT. RAD LAB, BERKELEY – DAY

I look down onto the bustle of students. Lomanitz looks up and
waves – then is ERASED by WHITEWASH as workers COVER the
windows . . . Serber hands me a key.

SERBER

This is the only key. Teller's here already. Shall I show him
in?

OPPENHEIMER

No, wait for the others –

The door BURSTS OPEN and a stooped, slightly heavy young man shuffles in. This is EDWARD TELLER.

> TELLER

Let's get started.

> OPPENHEIMER

Hello, Edward.

INT. SAME – DAY

I sit at the front, one long leg tucked under my ass. The scientists include Lawrence, Serber, Teller, BETHE, Condon, Tolman, Feynman, Donald, Bainbridge, NEDDERMEYER and Alvarez.

> OPPENHEIMER

We'll work here until the T-section at Los Alamos is finished –

I see Teller waving a piece of paper –

> OPPENHEIMER

Edward, can I get through my summary?

> TELLER

This is more important.

Teller's paper is passed around the room, scientists PALING . . .

> TELLER

Calculating chain reactions . . . I found a rather troubling possibility.

Hans Bethe hands me the paper, turns to Teller.

> BETHE

That can't be right. Show me how you did your calculations.

> TELLER

Of course.

I look up from the paper, grave. Teller watches the ruckus he's caused with evident satisfaction. Bethe approaches.

BETHE

Oppie, this is fantasy. Teller's calculations cannot be right.

OPPENHEIMER

Do them yourself while I go to Princeton.

BETHE

What for?

OPPENHEIMER

To talk to Einstein.

BETHE

There's not much common ground between you two.

OPPENHEIMER

That's why I should get his view.

EXT. WOODS, PRINCETON, NEW JERSEY – DAY

I walk through the trees, gaining on two figures. The two men turn. One them is Einstein.

EINSTEIN

Dr Oppenheimer. Have you met Kurt Gödel? We walk here most days.

GÖDEL

Trees are the most inspiring structures.

OPPENHEIMER

Albert, might I have a word?

Einstein senses the gravity. Nods. They leave Gödel staring up at the bare trees.

EINSTEIN

Some days Kurt refuses to eat. Even in Princeton, he's convinced the Nazis can poison his food.

EXT. LAKE, INSTITUTE FOR ADVANCED STUDY –
MOMENTS LATER

Einstein and I emerge from the trees. I pull a piece of paper from
my breast pocket. Einstein takes it.

> EINSTEIN
> Who's work is this?

> OPPENHEIMER
> Teller.

> EINSTEIN
> And what do you take it to mean?

> OPPENHEIMER
> Neutron smashes into nucleus releasing neutrons to smash
> into other nuclei . . .

INSERT CUT: DARKNESS SPLIT BY GLOWING PARTICLES FIRING
INTO EACH OTHER IN AN INCREASINGLY VIOLENT DISPLAY . . .

> OPPENHEIMER
> Criticality – the point of no return – massive explosive
> force . . . but the chain reaction *doesn't stop* . . .

Einstein studies the paper . . . he nods.

> EINSTEIN
> It would ignite the atmosphere.

The air around us CATCHES FIRE . . . THE PLANET EARTH, LONELY
IN VAST DARKNESS, IS SUDDENLY ENGULFED IN FIRE.

> OPPENHEIMER
> When we detonate an atomic device, we might start a
> chain reaction that destroys the world.

> EINSTEIN
> And here we are, lost in your quantum world of
> probabilities, but needing certainty.

> OPPENHEIMER
> Can you run the calculations yourself?

                    EINSTEIN
About the only thing you and I share is a disdain for
mathematics. Who's working on it at Berkeley?

                    OPPENHEIMER
Hans Bethe.

                    OPPENHEIMER
He'll get to the truth.

                    EINSTEIN
And if the truth is catastrophic?

                    EINSTEIN
Then you stop. And share your findings with the Nazis, so
neither side destroys the world.

I turn to leave.

                    EINSTEIN
Robert?
            (holding out paper)
This is yours. Not mine.

INT. CORRIDOR, BERKELEY – DAY

I come past the secretaries. Bethe is there, excited.

                    BETHE
Teller's wrong –

I gesture SILENCE as I unlock the Rad Lab –

INT. RAD LAB, BERKELEY – CONTINUOUS

Bethe runs to the cabinet – takes out some papers – hands them
to me, excited. I start to scan them, GRINNING –

                    BETHE
When you narrow Teller's critical assumptions the real
picture emerges –

OPPENHEIMER

Bottom line?

BETHE

The chances of an uncontrolled nuclear reaction are near zero.

OPPENHEIMER

Near zero?

BETHE

Oppie, this is good news –

OPPENHEIMER

Can you run more calculations?

BETHE

You'll get the same answer. Until we actually detonate one of these things, the best assurance you're going to get is this –

(jabs paper)

Near zero.

OPPENHEIMER

Theory will take you only so far.

INT. OPPENHEIMER HOUSE, BERKELEY – NIGHT

Kitty opens the door to the Chevaliers, finger to her lips – I am holding the sleeping Peter.

BARBARA
(whispering)

So beautiful. We miss him.

KITTY

Want to adopt?

OPPENHEIMER

She's kidding.

Kitty shakes her head, 'not kidding'. Barbara takes Peter. I lead Chevalier to the kitchen . . .

OPPENHEIMER
We wanted to see you before we left.

CHEVALIER
For parts unknown . . .

INT. KITCHEN, OPPENHEIMER HOUSE, BERKELEY –
CONTINUOUS

I mix a tray of martinis. Chevalier watches, distracted.

CHEVALIER
You know who I ran into the other day? Eltenton.

OPPENHEIMER
The chemist from Shell? Union guy?

CHEVALIER
Yeah. He was moaning about the way we're handling the war.

OPPENHEIMER
How so?

CHEVALIER
Lack of cooperation with our allies. Apparently, our government isn't sharing any research with the Russians. He said a lot of scientists think the policy's stupid.

My hands SLOW . . .

OPPENHEIMER
Oh, yeah?

CHEVALIER
Yeah. He mentioned that if anyone had information they wanted to pass on, going around official channels, he could help . . .

I look up at Chevalier. Grave.

OPPENHEIMER
That would be treason.

CHEVALIER
Yes, of course. I just thought you should know.

We STARE at each other . . . BANG – Kitty barges in.

KITTY
Brat's down – where are the martinis?

She sees us having a moment . . .

OPPENHEIMER
(V.O.)
The discussion ended there.

I pick up the tray.

INT. ROOM 2022, ATOMIC ENERGY COMMISSION –
DAY

OPPENHEIMER
Nothing in our long-standing friendship would have
led me to believe that Chevalier was actually seeking
information; and I was certain he had no idea of the work
on which I was engaged.

I steal a glance at Robb, then look directly at the board –

OPPENHEIMER
It has long been clear to me that I should have reported
this incident at once.

SENATOR McGEE
(V.O.)
The Oppenheimer situation highlights the tension between
scientists and the security apparatus . . .

Cut to:

INT. SENATE COMMITTEE HEARING ROOM – DAY
(B & W)

Strauss is at the witness table facing the Senate Committee.

                    SENATOR McGEE
*In hopes of learning how the nominee handled such issues
during his time at the AEC, we'll have a scientist appearing
before the Committee.*

                    STRAUSS
                    (private)
Who're they bringing in?

                    COUNSEL
                    (private)
They haven't said.

                    STRAUSS
*Mr Chairman, if I may? I'm nominated for Commerce
Secretary. Why seek the opinion of scientists –*

                    CHAIRMAN
*This is a Cabinet post, Admiral. We seek a wide range of
opinion.*

                    STRAUSS
*I'd like to know the name of the scientist testifying. And I'd
like the chance to cross-examine.*

                    CHAIRMAN
                    (irritated)
This is not a court.

INT. SENATE OFFICE – MOMENTS LATER (B&W)

The Senate Aide shows Strauss and Counsel in.

                    COUNSEL
Lewis, you're not on trial –

                    STRAUSS
So everyone keeps saying.

                    COUNSEL
*You act like a defence attorney, the Committee's gonna act
like a prosecutor.*

STRAUSS
(to Senate Aide)

A formality, huh?

SENATE AIDE

*No Presidential Cabinet nominee has failed to be
confirmed since 1925. This is just how the game is played.*

COUNSEL

*It's in the bag, Lewis, so play nice. They bring in a scientist,
so what?*

Strauss gives a wry smile. Remembers –

INSERT CUT: STRAUSS APPROACHES EINSTEIN AND OPPENHEIMER –
EINSTEIN BLOWS PAST WITHOUT ACKNOWLEDGING STRAUSS . . .

STRAUSS

*You don't know scientists like I do, counselor. They resent
anyone who questions their judgement – especially if
you're not one of them . . .*

INSERT CUT: STRAUSS STARES – THE CROWD AT THE ISOTOPES
HEARING LAUGHS . . .

STRAUSS

*I was chair of the AEC – I'm easy to blame for what
happened to Robert.*

SENATE AIDE

*We can't let the Senate think that the scientific community
doesn't support you.*

STRAUSS

Should we pivot?

SENATE AIDE

To what?

STRAUSS

Embrace it. 'I fought Oppenheimer and the US won'?

SENATE AIDE

I don't think we need to go there. Isn't there anyone we can call who knows what really happened?

STRAUSS

Teller.

SENATE AIDE

He'll make an impression.

STRAUSS

Can you find out the name of the scientist they've called?

SENATE AIDE

Probably.

STRAUSS
(to Counsel)
We get that name – you call the AEC, find out if he was based in Chicago or Los Alamos during the war.

SENATE AIDE

Why's that matter?

STRAUSS

If he was in Chicago he worked under Szilard and Fermi, not the cult of Oppie at Los Alamos. Robert built that damn place – he was founder, mayor, sheriff all rolled into one . . .

Cut to:

INT./EXT. CAR DRIVING THROUGH LOS ALAMOS – DAY (COLOUR)

I DRIVE Kitty and Peter through the 'town' . . . Kitty STARES at the newly built BASIC WOODEN STRUCTURES . . .

KITTY

All it needs is a saloon.

INT. OPPENHEIMER HOUSE, LOS ALAMOS – DAY

I stand in the hall, holding Peter, NERVOUS, as Kitty inspects the house . . . she pokes her head back in –

KITTY

Robert. There's no kitchen.

OPPENHEIMER

Really? We'll fix that. Don't worry.

EXT. T-SECTION, LOS ALAMOS – DAY

I walk Bethe through the security gate.

BETHE

Barbed wire. Guns, Oppie.

OPPENHEIMER

We're at war, Hans.

INT. LECTURE HALL, T-SECTION, LOS ALAMOS – DAY

I step up to join Serber – throw up a slide. Condon, Neddermeyer, Kistiakowsky, Donald, Tolman, Bainbridge and Feynman, amongst other SCIENTISTS, are in attendance.

OPPENHEIMER

Halifax, 1917. A cargo ship carrying munitions exploded in the harbor . . .

INSERT CUT: WOOD AND CONCRETE FRAGMENTS AND FLIES . . .

OPPENHEIMER

A vast and sudden chemical reaction . . .

INSERT CUT: A SHOCKWAVE DRIFTS ACROSS THE TOPS OF THE CHOPPY WATER . . .

OPPENHEIMER

The biggest man-made explosion in history. Let's calculate how much more destructive it would have been with a

nuclear, not chemical, reaction. Expressing power in terms
of tons of TNT –

> BETHE

But it'll be thousands.

> OPPENHEIMER

Then, *kilo*tons.

I switch the lights on, step down to let Serber –

> SERBER

Using U-235, the bomb –

He sees me wave.

> SERBER

Sorry – the *gadget* will need a thirty-three-pound sphere,
about this size . . .

Serber reaches below the table, brings up a GOLDFISH BOWL –

> SERBER

Or using plutonium, a ten-pound sphere . . .

He puts a large BRANDY GLASS next to the aquarium.

> SERBER

Here's the amount of uranium Oak Ridge refined all of last
month.

Serber drops THREE MARBLES into the bowl. The scientists stare
at the almost-empty goldfish bowl.

> SERBER

The Hanford plant made this much plutonium . . .

He drops TWO MARBLES into the brandy glass.

> SERBER

If we can enrich these amounts . . . we need a way to
detonate them.

Teller is at the back folding a paper plane.

OPPENHEIMER
Are we boring you, Edward?

TELLER
(without looking up)
Yes.

OPPENHEIMER
May I ask why?

TELLER
We came *into* this room knowing a fission bomb was
possible. Let's leave it with something new.

OPPENHEIMER
Such as?

TELLER
A 'super' atomic bomb. Instead of uranium, or plutonium,
we use hydrogen.

MURMURS of dissent –

TELLER
(shutting them down)
Heavy hydrogen – deuterium. We compact the atoms
together under great force and induce a *fusion* reaction.
Not kilotons . . . *mega*tons.

A HUBBUB develops – I process quickly, then –

OPPENHEIMER
Hang on. How do you generate enough force to fuse
hydrogen atoms?

Teller smiles a self-satisfied smile.

TELLER
A small fission bomb.

GROANS all around . . .

OPPENHEIMER

Well, since you're going to need one, anyway . . . can we get back to the business at hand?

Teller SHRUGS.

INT. SENATE COMMITTEE HEARING ROOM – DAY (B&W)

SENATOR BARTLETT

Mr Strauss, the isotopes issue wasn't your most important policy disagreement with Dr Oppenheimer. It was the Hydrogen bomb, wasn't it?

STRAUSS

We did disagree about the need for an H-bomb programme.

SENATOR BARTLETT

Tell us how that came to pass.

As Strauss REMEMBERS *we hear a* SIREN *and we –*

Cut to:

EXT. NEW YORK STREET – NIGHT (B&W)

Strauss is in a car, barrelling along behind a POLICE ESCORT *–*

INT. HOTEL, NEW YORK – NIGHT (B&W)

Strauss and his ASSISTANT *rush down the corridor to a door –*

INT. HOTEL CONFERENCE ROOM – NIGHT (B&W)

Strauss enters – a table surrounded by AEC members – Oppenheimer is slouched at the table, pipe blazing, Bush presides . . . Strauss removes his overcoat, revealing a tuxedo . . .

STRAUSS

What do we know?

                              BUSH
One of our B-29s over the north Pacific picked up
radiation.

Rabi uses a compass to indicate an area on the map . . .

                            STRAUSS
Do you have the filter papers?

                         OPPENHEIMER
There's no doubt what this is.

                            STRAUSS
The White House says there's doubt.

Oppenheimer begrudgingly slides them over to Strauss.

                              BUSH
Wishful thinking, I'm afraid.

                         OPPENHEIMER
It's an atomic test.

                            STRAUSS
The Soviets have a bomb? We're supposed to be years
ahead of them. What were you guys doing at Los Alamos?
Wasn't the security tight?

                         OPPENHEIMER
Of course it was – you weren't there, Lewis.

                            NICHOLS
                             (O.S.)
Forgive me, doctor . . .

Strauss leans around the FLOWERS in the centre of the table to
see who is speaking – Nichols, now a civilian.

But I _was_ there.

Cut to:

84

EXT. T-SECTION, LOS ALAMOS – DAY (COLOUR)

Condon, Nichols and I watch cars pull up. Groves emerges.

> OPPENHEIMER
> Welcome back.

> GROVES
> Progress?

INSERT CUT: MARBLES DROP INTO THE GOLDFISH BOWL.

> OPPENHEIMER
> It's nice to see you, too.

> GROVES
> Meet the British contingent.

SCIENTISTS emerge. A THIN YOUNG MAN offers his hand –

> FUCHS
> (German accent)
> Dr Oppenheimer, Klaus Fuchs.

> OPPENHEIMER
> How long have *you* been British?

> FUCHS
> Since Hitler told me I wasn't German.

INT. LECTURE HALL, T-SECTION, LOS ALAMOS – DAY

Bethe, Teller, Condon, Kistiakowsky, Donald, Bainbridge, Fuchs and Feynman and other scientists listen to –

> SERBER
> I call it 'shooting' – we fire a chunk of fissionable material into the larger sphere with enough force to achieve criticality.

INSERT CUT: A URANIUM 'BULLET' IS FIRED INTO A SPHERE –

TOLMAN

I've been thinking about implosion. Explosives around the sphere blast inwards, crushing the material.

INSERT CUT: A SPHERICAL ARRAY OF EXPLOSIVES BLASTS INWARD –

NEDDERMEYER

I'd like to investigate that idea.

OPPENHEIMER

I'll talk to the Ordinance division – we'll get you blowing things up . . .

EXT. 'MAIN STREET', LOS ALAMOS – DAY

Condon, Nichols and I show Groves the GROWING TOWN . . .

OPPENHEIMER

School's up and running. I thought of a way to reduce support staff . . .

I open the door to the cabin containing my office –

INT. OUTER OFFICE – CONTINUOUS

Groves notices the YOUNG WOMAN working behind the desk –

INT. OPPENHEIMER'S OFFICE, LOS ALAMOS – CONTINUOUS

I slump into my chair. Groves is perplexed –

GROVES

Is that . . .?

OPPENHEIMER

Mrs Serber. I've offered jobs to all the wives. Admin, librarians, computation. We cut down on staff and keep families together.

86

GROVES

Are these women qualified?

OPPENHEIMER

Don't be absurd. These are some of the brightest minds in our community.

CONDON

And they're already security cleared.

NICHOLS

I've informed General Groves you've been holding cross-divisional open discussions –

GROVES

Shut 'em down. Compartmentalization is the key to maintaining security –

NICHOLS

It's only the top men.

CONDON

Who, presumably, communicate with subordinates.

OPPENHEIMER

These men aren't stupid, they can be discreet.

GROVES

I don't like it.

OPPENHEIMER

You don't like anything enough for that to be a fair test.

Groves shrugs. Gets up to leave. Nichols rolls his eyes.

GROVES

Once a week. Top men only.

OPPENHEIMER

I'd like to bring my brother here.

GROVES

No.

Groves and Condon leave – I corner Nichols –

OPPENHEIMER

I still haven't heard that my security clearance has been
approved.

NICHOLS

It hasn't.

OPPENHEIMER

We're going to Chicago tomorrow –

NICHOLS

You should wait.

OPPENHEIMER

You're aware that the Nazis have a two-year head start?

NICHOLS

Dr Oppenheimer, the fact that your security clearance is
proving difficult to obtain is not my fault. It's yours.

OPPENHEIMER

It may not be your fault, but it's your problem. Because I'm
going.

Cut to:

INT. HOTEL CONFERENCE ROOM – NIGHT (B&W)

*Strauss reaches to the centre of the table to move the flowers
from between him and Nichols –*

STRAUSS

How many people were in the open discussions?

NICHOLS

*Too many. Compartmentalization was supposed to be the
protocol.*

OPPENHEIMER

We were in a race against the Nazis –

STRAUSS

Well, now the race is against the Soviets.

OPPENHEIMER

Only if <u>we</u> start it.

Strauss holds up the filter papers.

STRAUSS

Robert, they just fired the starting gun. What's the nature of the device they detonated?

OPPENHEIMER

The data indicates it may have been a plutonium implosion device.

STRAUSS

Like the one you built at Los Alamos?

Oppenheimer nods reluctantly . . .

STRAUSS

If the Soviets have a bomb, Truman needs to know what's next.

Bush nods. Oppenheimer looks incredulous –

OPPENHEIMER

What's next? Arms talks. Obviously.

STRAUSS

(to Bush)

What about the Super? Does Truman even know about it?

BUSH

Not specifically.

OPPENHEIMER

We still don't know if a Hydrogen bomb is technically feasible.

STRAUSS

My understanding is that Teller first proposed it at Los Alamos.

OPPENHEIMER
*His designs have always been wildly impractical. You'd
have to deliver by ox-cart not airplane.*

STRAUSS
*If it could put us ahead again, Truman needs to know
about it. And if there's a possibility that the Russians know
about it from a spy at Los Alamos . . . we've gotta get
going.*

OPPENHEIMER
There's no proof there was a spy at Los Alamos.

Strauss holds up the filter papers, raises his eyebrows . . .

Cut to:

EXT. FOOTBALL STADIUM, CHICAGO – DAY (COLOUR)

Condon and I are led across the field by J. Ernest WILKINS . . .

CONDON
They put it under the football stadium?

WILKINS
The field's not in use, anymore.

OPPENHEIMER
Just as well.

INT. ATOMIC PILE, UNDERNEATH THE STADIUM,
CHICAGO – DAY

Wilkins shows us to SZILARD and FERMI. A scientist with
GLASSES takes notes. The group approaches the atomic pile . . .

FERMI
I hear you've got a little town.

OPPENHEIMER
Come and see.

SZILARD

Who could think straight in a place like that? Everybody
will go crazy.

OPPENHEIMER

Thanks for the vote of confidence, Szilard.

I spot Glasses SCRIBBLING – I GRAB his pen – he FLINCHES –

OPPENHEIMER

We really need that in the notes?
(to Fermi)
When are you going to try it out?

FERMI

We already did. The first self-sustaining nuclear chain
reaction. Didn't Groves tell you?

EXT. T-SECTION, LOS ALAMOS – DAY

Condon and I have just passed through –

HORNIG

Dr Oppenheimer! I tried personnel.

We turn to see a twenty-three-year-old young woman on the
other side of the barrier. This is Lilli HORNIG.

HORNIG

They asked if I could type.

OPPENHEIMER

Can you?

HORNIG

Harvard forgot to teach that on the graduate chemistry
course.

I smile at this. Turn to Condon.

OPPENHEIMER

Put Mrs Hornig on the plutonium team.

INT. CYCLOTRON BUILDING, LOS ALAMOS –
CONTINUOUS

Condon and I peer up at the equipment. Groves STORMS in –

GROVES
What the hell were you doing in Chicago?!

CONDON
Visiting the Met Lab –

GROVES
Why?!

Condon looks at me. I say nothing. He turns to Groves –

CONDON
You can't talk to us like this. We have every right –

GROVES
You have just the rights I give you! No more, no less.

CONDON
This is ridiculous – we're adults, trying to run a project
here.
                    (to me)
Tell him, Robert.

I look steadily at Groves.

OPPENHEIMER
Compartmentalization is the protocol we agreed to.

CONDON
You've got to be kidding me. Enough of this madhouse –
nobody can work under these conditions.
                    (to Groves)
You know what, Generalissimo? I quit.
                    (to Oppenheimer)
Thanks for nothing.

Condon storms out. Groves turns to me.

GROVES

Better off without him.

OPPENHEIMER

Aren't you more worried about his discretion out there?

GROVES

We'll have him killed.
                    (off Oppenheimer's look)
Kidding. He hates me, not America.

OPPENHEIMER

Not everyone has levers like mine to pull.

GROVES

I don't know what you mean.

OPPENHEIMER

You didn't hire me *despite* my left-wing past, you hired me *because* of it. So you could control me.

GROVES

I'm not that subtle. I'm just a humble soldier.

OPPENHEIMER

You're neither humble, nor 'just' a soldier. You studied engineering at MIT.

OPPENHEIMER

Guilty as charged.

GROVES

Now that we understand each other, perhaps you'll get me my security clearance, so I can perform this miracle for you.

General Groves looks at me. Nods.

GARRISON
(V.O.)

General Groves, were you aware of Dr Oppenheimer's left-wing associations when you appointed him?

INT. ROOM 2022, ATOMIC ENERGY COMMISSION –
DAY

Groves, in CIVILIAN CLOTHES, testifies. I watch . . .

> GROVES
> I was aware that there were suspicions about him . . . I was
> aware that he had a very extreme liberal background.

> GARRISON
> In your opinion, would he ever consciously commit a
> disloyal act?

> GROVES
> I would be amazed if he did.

> GARRISON
> You had complete confidence in his integrity?

> GROVES
> At Los Alamos, yes, which is where I really knew him.

> ROBB
> General, did your security officers on the project advise
> against the clearance of Dr Oppenheimer?

> GROVES
> Truer to say they could not and would not clear him. Until
> I insisted.

> ROBB
> You became pretty familiar with the security file on
> Dr Oppenheimer?

> GROVES
> I did.

> ROBB
> General, there's really only one question we need answered
> here today . . .

Groves shifts, knowing what's about to be asked . . .

                              ROBB
In the light of your experience of security matters and
knowledge of the file . . .

EXT. T-SECTION, LOS ALAMOS – DAY

I greet Lawrence and Lomanitz as they get out of a car –

                              ROBB
                             (V.O.)
. . . would you clear Dr Oppenheimer today?

                           LAWRENCE
Physics and New Mexico, huh? But my God, what a trek.

                         OPPENHEIMER
That's why you need a liaison.

                           LAWRENCE
I'm appointing Lomanitz.

I pat Lomanitz on the shoulder.

                         OPPENHEIMER
You're gonna be okay.

INT. LECTURE HALL, T-SECTION, LOS ALAMOS – LATER

As the group assembles, General Groves speaks to Lawrence.

                            GROVES
I'll remind you what we talked about in Berkeley, doctor.

                           LAWRENCE
Compartmentalization. I understand completely.

Oppenheimer theatrically drops three marbles into the quarter-
full goldfish bowl, then ADDS TWO MORE – the room APPLAUDS.
Oppenheimer BOWS, steps down. Lawrence BOUNCES up –

LAWRENCE

Greetings from Berkeley. I'm here to update you on our
progress and solicit your input. To do so I will be sharing
many things that General Groves has told me not to . . .
(to Groves)
Well, General, I said I 'understood', not that I agreed. So,
to business . . .

Groves looks at me. I shrug. He leaves.

Cut to:

INT. HOTEL CONFERENCE ROOM – NIGHT (B&W)

Strauss places the filter papers back down on the table . . .

STRAUSS

There <u>were</u> reports of espionage from Los Alamos –

OPPENHEIMER

Unsubstantiated reports –

STRAUSS

*I've heard there were Communists on the project – were
any of them involved with discussions of the Super?*

OPPENHEIMER

We didn't knowingly employ any Communists.

NICHOLS

*I seem to remember you demanding that your brother
come to Los Alamos.*

OPPENHEIMER

He'd left the Party by then.

STRAUSS

And Lomanitz?

OPPENHEIMER

*He was never employed at Los Alamos, he was a liaison.
Our security was tight, as former Colonel Nichols well
knows.*

Our security was the tightest we could make it given the personalities involved. But attempts <u>were</u> made. Doctor, we've all read your file here. Do we need to talk about Jean Tatlock? Or the Chevalier incident?

Strauss watches Oppenheimer glare at Nichols.

Cut to:

INT. OPPENHEIMER'S OFFICE, LOS ALAMOS – DAY (COLOUR)

SECRETARY
(over intercom)
That's Lomanitz on one . . .

I pick up the phone –

OPPENHEIMER
Lomanitz? Okay, hang on, calm down.

INT. COLONEL NICHOLS' OFFICE – MOMENTS LATER

I stand at Nichols' desk.

OPPENHEIMER
There's been another screw-up – Lomanitz just got drafted.

NICHOLS
We *are* at war, doctor.

OPPENHEIMER
Don't be an asshole, Nichols. We need this kid. Fix it, will you?

NICHOLS
It wasn't a mistake. Your friend Lomanitz has been trying to unionize the Radiation Lab.

OPPENHEIMER
He promised to quit all that.

                    NICHOLS
Well, he hasn't. The security officer at Berkeley is
concerned about Communist infiltration through that
union – the . . . F-A . . .

                    OPPENHEIMER
                    (thinking)
F-A-E-C-T. I'm there next week, maybe I'll drop in to see
him.

Nichols TOSSES a security pass across the desk.

                    NICHOLS
Your Q clearance came through. It's important you not
maintain or renew any questionable associations.

                    ROBB
                    (V.O.)
Doctor, did you think social contacts between a person
employed on secret war work and Communists was
dangerous?

INT. ROOM 2022, ATOMIC ENERGY COMMISSION –
DAY

I testify, Kitty behind me . . .

                    OPPENHEIMER
My awareness of the danger would be greater today.

                    ROBB
But it's fair to say that during the war years . . .

EXT. HOTEL, SAN FRANCISCO – DAY

A TAXI pulls up. I get out, carrying a bag.

                    ROBB
                    (V.O.)
. . . you felt that such contacts were potentially dangerous?

I enter, without seeing a CAR FOLLOWING. The PASSENGER jumps out, while the DRIVER checks the time, makes a note.

INT. HOTEL LOBBY, SAN FRANCISCO – CONTINUOUS

> OPPENHEIMER
> (V.O.)
> Were *conceivably* dangerous.

I move to the elevators, watched by the passenger.

INT. CORRIDOR, HOTEL, SAN FRANCISCO –
CONTINUOUS

At the door to 805 I reach into my bag . . .

> ROBB
> (V.O.)
> Really? *Known* Communists?

. . . and remove a small BUNCH OF FLOWERS. I knock . . .

> OPPENHEIMER
> (V.O.)
> Look, I've had a lot of secrets in my head a long time. It doesn't matter who I associate with . . .

The door opens to reveal JEAN TATLOCK.

INT. ROOM 2022, ATOMIC ENERGY COMMISSION –
DAY

> OPPENHEIMER
> I don't talk about those secrets.

INT. ROOM 805, HOTEL, SAN FRANCISCO –
CONTINUOUS

Tatlock GRABS the flowers. As I follow her in, she DUMPS them in the wastebasket . . .

INT. ROOM 2022, ATOMIC ENERGY COMMISSION –
DAY

Robb refers to his papers – Kitty watches . . .

> ROBB
> You said in your statement you 'had' to visit Jean Tatlock
> in 1943 . . .

INT. ROOM 805, HOTEL, SAN FRANCISCO – NIGHT

Tatlock and I sit across the room from each other, naked.

> TATLOCK
> You left. Not a word. What did you think that would do to
> me?

> OPPENHEIMER
> I wrote.

> TATLOCK
> Pages of nothing. Where'd you go?

> OPPENHEIMER
> I can't tell you.

> TATLOCK
> Why not?

> OPPENHEIMER
> Because you're a Communist.

> ROBB
> (V.O.)
> Why did you *have* to see her?

INT. ROOM 2022, ATOMIC ENERGY COMMISSION –
DAY

I sit at the table, self-conscious, testifying . . .

OPPENHEIMER

She had indicated a great desire to see me before we left. At that time I couldn't. But I felt that she had to see me . . .

Kitty watches me testify. I am NAKED . . .

OPPENHEIMER

She was undergoing psychiatric treatment. She was extremely unhappy.

ROBB

Did you find out why she had to see you?

OPPENHEIMER

Because she was still in love with me.

Kitty watches Tatlock, also naked, STRADDLE me, head on my shoulder, facing Kitty . . .

ROBB

You spent the night with her didn't you?

As Tatlock GRINDS on me she locks eyes with Kitty . . .

OPPENHEIMER

Yes.

INT. ROOM 805, HOTEL, SAN FRANCISCO – NIGHT

Tatlock studies me from across the room.

TATLOCK

You drop in and out of my life and don't have to tell me why. That's power.

OPPENHEIMER

Not that I enjoy. I'd rather be here for you as you need.

TATLOCK

But now you've got other priorities.

OPPENHEIMER

I have a wife and child.

                          TATLOCK
      That's not what either of us is talking about.

                        OPPENHEIMER
      Jean, you asked me to come. And I'm glad I did. But I can't
      come again.

                          TATLOCK
      What if I need you?

I slowly shake my head.

                          TATLOCK
      Not a word?

INT. ROOM 2022, ATOMIC ENERGY COMMISSION –
DAY

All eyes on me, clothed and alone again . . .

                           ROBB
      Did you think that consistent with good security?

Behind me, Kitty's face is stone . . .

                        OPPENHEIMER
      It was, as a matter of fact. Not a word.

                           ROBB
      When did you see her after that?

INSERT CUT: HOT BATH RUNNING. PILL BOTTLE. DOWNTURNED
HEAD IN THE WATER. THE SOUND OF FEET STAMPING,
STAMPING . . .

I JAM my eyes closed, shake off the image –

                        OPPENHEIMER
      I never saw her again.

INT. SAME – DAY

As the room breaks up, Kitty speaks privately to me through CLENCHED TEETH as she gathers her things. No eye contact.

KITTY
I can make the last train back to Princeton.

OPPENHEIMER
I said nothing that I hadn't already said to you, Kitty.

KITTY
Well, today you said it to history.

OPPENHEIMER
This is a closed hearing –

KITTY
If they don't release a transcript, you will!

She DROPS her bag, spilling the contents. Garrison spots a small FLASK as Kitty sweeps it into her purse. I CROUCH –

OPPENHEIMER
I was under oath.

KITTY
You were under an oath to me when you went to see Jean.

She STANDS – I follow – she TURNS back – in my face –

KITTY
You sit there, day after day, letting them pick our lives to pieces. Why won't you fight?

I don't answer. She leaves. Garrison steps up.

GARRISON
Robert, I'm not putting her up there.

EXT. BERKELEY CAMPUS – DAY

I stroll across the campus, enter an administrative building.

INT. LT. JOHNSON'S OFFICE – MOMENTS LATER

I knock. Johnson opens the door, SURPRISED.

> JOHNSON
> Dr Oppenheimer, it's an honour. Please, take a seat –

> OPPENHEIMER
> No need. I just wanted to check whether I should talk to
> Lomanitz while I'm here – given your concerns.

> JOHNSON
> That's up to you, really, professor. But I'd be cautious.

> OPPENHEIMER
> Understood. Oh, and as far as the union goes, I wanted to
> give you a heads up on a man named Eltenton.

> JOHNSON
> A heads up?

> OPPENHEIMER
> He might merit watching, is all.

> JOHNSON
> I'd love to get more details –

> OPPENHEIMER
> I've got an appointment now, and I leave early tomorrow –

> JOHNSON
> Come as early as you like. Since you haven't time now.

> GROVES
> (V.O.)
> You went back the next morning?

INT. TRAIN, SANTA FE TO CHICAGO – DAY

Groves sits opposite. I stare out the window.

> OPPENHEIMER
> I did. I had to, really.

INT. LT. JOHNSON'S OFFICE – MORNING

Johnson smiles, beckons me in. Indicates a SECOND MAN –

                    OPPENHEIMER
                    (V.O.)
          This time there was another man.

INT. TRAIN, SANTA FE TO CHICAGO – DAY

I stare out the window. Groves sits opposite.

                    OPPENHEIMER
          Said his name was Pash.

                    GROVES
          Pash? You met Colonel Pash?

INT. ROOM 2022, ATOMIC ENERGY COMMISSION –
DAY

Alone on the couch, I glance up, NERVOUS, as a man in uniform
walks past. As he sits, I study the back of his head.

                    ROBB
          Colonel Pash, can you read from your memo of June 29th,
          1943?

                    PASH
          'Results of surveillance conducted on subject indicate
          further possible Communist Party connections. Subject met
          with and spent considerable time with one Jean Tatlock,
          Communist, the record of whom is attached.'

                    ROBB
          The subject being Dr Oppenheimer?

                    PASH
          Yes.

                    ROBB
          Whom you had not met?

PASH
Not then, but soon after . . .

INT. TRAIN, SANTA FE TO CHICAGO – DAY

OPPENHEIMER
He's head of security for the project, shouldn't I know him?

GROVES
No, he should know you. I'd never put you in a room with Pash.

OPPENHEIMER
Why not?

GROVES
When Pash first learned about Lomanitz – he told the FBI he was going to kidnap him, take him out on a boat, interrogate him 'in the Russian manner' . . .

INT. LT. JOHNSON'S OFFICE – DAY

Pash sits down next to me, opposite Johnson.

PASH
Dr Oppenheimer, this is a pleasure. General Groves has placed a certain responsibility in me, and it's like having a child, that you can't see, by remote control, so to actually meet you . . . I don't mean to take much of your time . . .

The disarming friendliness of the truly dangerous.

OPPENHEIMER
Not at all. Whatever time you choose.

PASH
Mr Johnson told me of your conversation yesterday, in which I'm very interested. It had me worried all day . . .

OPPENHEIMER
I didn't want to talk to Lomanitz without authorization –

PASH

That's not the particular interest I have. It's something a
little more, in my opinion, more serious . . .

INT. TRAIN, SANTA FE TO CHICAGO – DAY

GROVES

When the FBI pointed out that such information couldn't
be used in court Pash made it clear that he didn't intend to
have anyone left to prosecute. The FBI talked him down,
but that's the man you're dancing with.

INT. LT. JOHNSON'S OFFICE – DAY

PASH

I gather you've heard there are other parties interested in
the work of the Radiation Lab . . .

OPPENHEIMER

Well, a man attached to the Soviet Consul indicated,
through intermediate people, to people on this project that
he was in a position to transmit information they might
supply.

PASH

Why would anyone on the project want that?

OPPENHEIMER

Frankly, I can see there might be arguments for the
commander-in-chief informing the Russians – they're our
allies. But I don't like the idea of it going out the back
door – it might not hurt to be on the lookout for it.

INT. TRAIN, SANTA FE TO CHICAGO – DAY

GROVES

You said that to Pash?

OPPENHEIMER

I was trying to put it in the context of . . . Russia's not
Germany.

GROVES

Boris Pash is the son of a Russian Orthodox bishop. Born
here, but in 1918 he went back to Russia to fight the
Bolsheviks. This is a man who's killed Communists with
his own hands.

INT. LT. JOHNSON'S OFFICE – DAY

Pash spreads his palms . . .

PASH

I'm not the judge of who should or should not get
information. My business is to stop it going through
illegally. Could you be a little more specific?

OPPENHEIMER

There's a man whose name was mentioned to me a couple
of times – Eltenton. I think he's a chemist employed by
Shell. He talked to a friend of his who's an acquaintance
of someone on the project. To go beyond that would be to
put names down of people who are not only innocent but
were one hundred percent cooperative.

INT. TRAIN, SANTA FE TO CHICAGO – DAY

Groves is staring at me like I just crapped my pants.

GROVES

You thought Pash would be satisfied with that?

OPPENHEIMER

I was trying to give them Eltenton without opening a can
of worms. I told him a cock-and-bull story.

INT. ROOM 2022, ATOMIC ENERGY COMMISSION –
DAY

I am up front. Robb questioning –

> ROBB
> Did you lie to General Groves, too?

> OPPENHEIMER
> No, I told him I'd lied to Pash.

INT. SAME – DAY

Groves is on the stand, in civilian clothes –

> GARRISON
> Do you recall your conversation with him about the
> Chevalier incident?

> GROVES
> I've seen so many versions of it, I wasn't confused before,
> but I'm certainly getting there now.

> GARRISON
> What was your conclusion?

> GROVES
> That he was under the influence of the typical American
> schoolboy attitude that there's something wicked about
> telling on a friend. He did what he thought was essential –
> disclosing Eltenton.

INT. SAME – DAY

Pash is testifying.

> PASH
> The memo I wrote at the time states 'Dr Oppenheimer
> sought to provide information to burnish his image as
> loyal, clearly having heard of our investigation at Berkeley.
> He is not to be trusted on matters of security.'

INT. LT. JOHNSON'S OFFICE – DAY

Pash gazes, unblinking, into my eyes . . .

> PASH
>
> These other people you mentioned, were they contacted by Eltenton direct?

> OPPENHEIMER
>
> No.

> PASH
>
> Well now, could we know through whom that contact was made?

> OPPENHEIMER
>
> It would involve people who ought not be involved in this.

> PASH
>
> Is this person a member of the project?

> OPPENHEIMER
>
> A member of the faculty, but not on the project.

> PASH
>
> Eltenton made the approach through a member of the faculty here at Berkeley?

> OPPENHEIMER
>
> As far as I know – there may have been more than one person involved. If I seem uncooperative I think you can understand that it's because of my insistence in not getting innocent people into trouble.

Pash stares at me. I finally keep my mouth shut.

> PASH
>
> You see me as persistent –

> OPPENHEIMER
>
> You are persistent, and that is your job. But my job is protecting the people who work for me.

PASH

Instead of us going on certain steps which may come to
your attention and be a little bit . . . *disturbing* to you . . .
I'd rather discuss those with you first. I'm not formulating
any plans, I'm just going to have to digest the whole thing.

I nod at Pash. Get to my feet.

INT. TRAIN, SANTA FE TO CHICAGO – DAY

Groves takes in the story.

GROVES

You're protecting a friend. But who's protecting you?

OPPENHEIMER

You could.

GROVES

If you gave me the name.

OPPENHEIMER

If you order me to, I'll do it.

GROVES

You're making a mistake, Robert. A mistake that may
haunt you. You need to *volunteer* this name.

I turn to watch the scenery trundle past.

ROBB
(V.O.)

And did he give you the name?

INT. ROOM 2022, ATOMIC ENERGY COMMISSION –
DAY

GROVES

He did.

ROBB

But not at that time.

> GROVES

No.

> ROBB

In fact, it was some months later, wasn't it?

Groves nods.

INT. SAME – DAY

I study the back of Boris Pash's head . . .

> ROBB

And in the months between your interview with
Dr Oppenheimer and his eventual naming of Chevalier,
did you expend resources trying to find the identity of the
intermediary?

> PASH

Considerable resources. Without the name our job was
extremely difficult.

> ROBB

When did you receive the name?

> PASH

I was gone by the time Oppenheimer offered it up.

> ROBB

Gone?

> PASH

They felt my time would be better spent in Europe
determining the status of the Nazi bomb project.

> ROBB

Who did?

> PASH

General Groves. He transferred me to London.

I lift my head at this.

INSERT CUT: MARBLES DROP INTO THE BOWL . . . THREE-QUARTERS FULL . . .

EXT. LOS ALAMOS – NIGHT

Serber and I walk down the street. Snow falling.

> SERBER
> Little early for a Christmas party.

> OPPENHEIMER
> Something's up. Tolman's been away.

> SERBER
> Where?

> OPPENHEIMER
> Ruth won't tell.

We head towards Fuller Lodge . . .

INT. FULLER LODGE, LOS ALAMOS – LATER

A CHRISTMAS PARTY. DEBAUCHED. Kitty, in SANTA HAT, serves/spikes the EGGNOG. Bethe, Teller, Charlotte Serber, Neddermeyer, Kistiakowsky, Donald, Hornig, Bainbridge, Fuchs, Feynman amongst the revelers. I have Ruth cornered, glancing over at Kitty, who pretends she wasn't looking at me and GRABS at the nearest male arm – pushing eggnog . . .

> RUTH
> Compartmentalization, Oppie. What makes you think
> I know, anyway?

I take *her* glass. Sip from it . . .

> OPPENHEIMER
> You do a good job of knowing where Mr Tolman is . . .
> when it counts.

> RUTH
> Like now.

I turn – Tolman and Groves enter, brushing off snow . . .

> GROVES
>
> Atten-shun! We have an early Christmas present for you . . .

They step aside to reveal . . . NIELS BOHR. I grin.

> BOHR
> (V.O.)
> The British pilots put me in the bomb bay . . .

INT. SAME – LATER

Bohr holds court. I listen at the back.

> BOHR
> . . . showed me the oxygen – of course I messed it up. When they opened me up in Scotland I was unconscious. I pretended I'd been napping.

The crowd LAUGHS, loving it. Bohr peels off to talk to me.

Is it big enough?

> OPPENHEIMER
> To end the war?

> BOHR
> To end *all* war.

INT. LECTURE HALL, T-SECTION – LATER

I sip my drink, watching Bohr read the boards. Tolman, Teller, Bethe and Serber sprawl, party hats, TINSEL scarves . . .

> BOHR
> Heisenberg sought me out in Copenhagen. It was chilling – my old student, working for the Nazis. He told me things to draw me out . . . sustained fission reactions in uranium . . .

TOLMAN

That sounds more like a reactor than a bomb.

TELLER

Did he mention gaseous diffusion?

BOHR

He seemed more focused on heavy water.

TELLER

As a moderator?

BOHR

Yes. Instead of graphite.

Serber and Tolman GRIN. I nod. Bohr notices us relax . . .

BOHR

What?

OPPENHEIMER

He took a wrong turn. We're ahead. And with you here to help us . . .

Bohr turns to Teller and the others –

BOHR

Gentlemen, could you give us a moment?

They shuffle out. Bohr looks at the MARBLES. Turns to me . . .

BOHR

I'm not here to help, Robert. I knew you could do this without me.

OPPENHEIMER

Then why did you come?

BOHR

To talk about *after*. The power you're revealing will forever outlive the Nazis. And the world is not prepared.

OPPENHEIMER

You can lift the rock without being ready for the snake that's revealed.

BOHR

We have to make the politicians understand – this isn't
a new weapon – it's a new world. I'll be out there, doing
what I can – but *you* . . .
(points at me)
You're an American Prometheus – Father of the Atomic
Bomb. The man who gave them the power to destroy
themselves. They'll respect that. And your work really
begins.

I take this in. Charlotte Serber enters –

CHARLOTTE

I'm sorry, Oppie, but there's a call. From San Francisco.

I look at my watch, surprised . . . look at Bohr, who nods 'Go.'

EXT. SNOWY WOODS, LOS ALAMOS – DAWN

Kitty, on horseback, finds my horse, tied up. She dismounts,
moving into the trees . . . She finds me curled up at the base of a
tree in the SNOW, distraught.

KITTY

Robert?

She crouches, touches my shoulder – I look up, ASHAMED.

OPPENHEIMER

Her father called . . . they found her yesterday . . . in the
bath . . .

INSERT CUT: A WOMAN, FACE-DOWN IN THE BATH, A CUSHION
BELOW . . .

KITTY

Who?

OPPENHEIMER

She'd taken pills, left a note . . . not signed . . . she took
barbiturates . . .

INSERT CUT: TATLOCK KNEELS IN THE BATH, POPPING PILLS. SINKS SERENELY ONTO CUSHIONS UNDER THE WATER . . .

OPPENHEIMER
But there was chloral hydrate in her blood . . .

INSERT CUT: GLOVED HANDS HOLDS TATLOCK'S STRUGGLING HEAD UNDERWATER . . .

I SHAKE OFF the image . . .

OPPENHEIMER
There was a note.

KITTY
Jean Tatlock?

INSERT CUT: OPPENHEIMER, NAKED, SHAKES HIS HEAD AT TATLOCK.

OPPENHEIMER
We were together – she said she needed me . . . but I told her I wouldn't see her again. It was me.

Kitty SLAPS me in the face. I look up at her, bleary-eyed . . .

KITTY
You don't get to commit the sin, then have us all feel sorry for you that it had consequences.
(rises)
Pull yourself together. People here depend on you.

INT. LECTURE HALL, T-SECTION, LOS ALAMOS – DAY

I vacantly preside over a shambles – the goldfish bowl is FILLED with marbles. As is the glass tumbler . . . Donald, Bainbridge, Feynman watch the others squabble –

HORNIG
Serber, I'm not quitting my job because plutonium's radioactive!

117

SERBER

We can't know what it might do to your reproductive
system – Donald, help me out, here –

DONALD

You're on your own, pal.

HORNIG
(to Serber)

Your reproductive system's more exposed than mine.
Presumably.

KISTIAKOWSKY

The implosion device is nowhere.

NEDDERMEYER

You can't rush everything, Oppie.

KISTIAKOWSKY

There's rushing and there's getting on with it – pick one,
will ya?

BETHE

Teller's not helping – I've been asking for calculations on
the implosion lenses for weeks –

TELLER

The British can do it – Fuchs –

FUCHS

Absolutely.

BETHE

It's *your* job, Teller!

TELLER

I'm engaged in research –

BETHE

On a Hydrogen bomb we're not even building!

Teller simply walks away. As he passes me –

TELLER

I won't work for that man.

118

                    BETHE
Let him go. He's a prima donna –

                    SERBER
I agree. He should leave Los Alamos.

I sigh. RISE, clear and direct –

                 OPPENHEIMER
Kisty, you replace Neddermeyer. Seth, I'm putting you on
plutonium. Lilli, go work for Kisty.
                 (off her look)
Because he needs you.
                    (to Fuchs)
Fuchs, take Teller's role – you're exclusively on the
implosion device.

I head for the door –

                 OPPENHEIMER
And *nobody* is leaving Los Alamos.

EXT. T-SECTION, LOS ALAMOS – DAY

Teller is held at the gate. I approach. We face off in the 'street'
like gunslingers.

                    TELLER
They won't let me leave.

                 OPPENHEIMER
I won't let you leave. Forget Hans, forget *fission*. Stay
here and research what you want. Fusion. The Hydrogen
bomb – whatever. We'll meet to discuss –

                    TELLER
You don't have time to meet. You're a politician now,
Robert. You left physics behind long ago.

                 OPPENHEIMER
Once a week. One hour, you and me.

Teller considers this. Nods, turns to the GUARD –

TELLER

Now, raise that fucking barrier.

ROBB
(O.S.)

So the Super was under development on your watch at Los Alamos . . .

INT. ROOM 2022, ATOMIC ENERGY COMMISSION –
DAY

ROBB

. . . yet, after the war, you tried to deny it was viable.

OPPENHEIMER

No. I pointed out technical difficulties with it.

ROBB

Didn't you try to kill it at the AEC meeting after the Russian bomb test?

OPPENHEIMER

No.

ROBB

But that *was* the recommendation the AEC offered, was it not?

OPPENHEIMER

After hours of discussion . . .

INT. HOTEL CONFERENCE ROOM – NIGHT (COLOUR)

Me, Bush, Nichols (CIVILIAN), Rabi, Fermi, Strauss and others.

OPPENHEIMER
(V.O.)

. . . about the best response.

BUSH

Truman *has* to do something . . .

Rabi opens his compasses wider . . .

RABI

An H-bomb would be one thousand times the power of an A-bomb.

He draws a circle around Moscow . . .

RABI

The only intended target would be the largest cities.

And a circle around St Petersburg . . .

RABI

It's a weapon of mass genocide.

STRAUSS

Why don't you draw some of those circles on this side of the map?

He points at the USA . . .

STRAUSS

Start here . . .
                    (gestures around them)
New York.

As I listen to them I hear the sound of FEET STAMPING . . .

FERMI

It's a weapon of attack, with no defensive value.

STRAUSS

Deterrence.

BUSH

Do we need more deterrence than our current arsenal of atomic bombs?

I tense up as the STAMPING SOUND gets LOUDER and LOUDER . . .

BUSH

Drown in ten feet of water or ten thousand, what's the difference? We can already drown Russia, and they know it.

INSERT CUT: DOZENS OF FEET STAMPING, FASTER AND FASTER . . .

STRAUSS

Now they can drown us.

INSERT CUT: . . . SO FAST THE FEET BREAK RHYTHM, CAUSING
CACOPHONY . . .

STRAUSS

Gentlemen, I have to ask whether your discussion should
be more of a technical one. Robert?

I JAM my eyes CLOSED, SHAKE OFF the image – the sound
STOPS –

OPPENHEIMER

Teller's designs are as impractical as they were during the
war.

LAWRENCE

The Hydrogen bomb can be made to work, Oppie. You
know that.

OPPENHEIMER

We can't commit all our resources to that chance.

STRAUSS

Then how would you have Truman reassure the American
people?

OPPENHEIMER

By limiting the spread of atomic weapons through
international control of nuclear energy.

STRAUSS

World government?

OPPENHEIMER

The United Nations. As Roosevelt intended.

STRAUSS

I asked what *Truman* should do. The world's changed.
Communism threatens our survival.

OPPENHEIMER

Lewis, if we build a Hydrogen bomb, the Soviets would
have no choice but to build their own.

STRAUSS

Could they be working on it already? Based on
information from a spy at Los Alamos?

OPPENHEIMER

There was no spy at Los Alamos!

BUSH

Gentlemen, let's not get sidetracked.

OPPENHEIMER

I say we use this moment to gain concessions from
the Russians by committing that we will not build the
Hydrogen bomb.

STRAUSS

Thereby revealing its existence.

OPPENHEIMER

Which you seem convinced they already know.

BUSH

At this point I'd like the Advisory Committee members to
meet in privacy to finalize our recommendations.

Strauss nods. Rises. Much of the room follows suit, leaving.

STRAUSS

I'm not sure you want to go down this road, Robert.

OPPENHEIMER

Lewis, we're the *Advisory* Committee. We'll give them our
advice.

Strauss shrugs. As he, Lawrence and Nichols leave together,
Borden approaches.

BORDEN

Dr Oppenheimer? William Borden – Joint Committee on
Atomic Energy.

OPPENHEIMER
Oh, yes.

BORDEN
During the war, I was a pilot. One night, flying back from a raid, I saw an amazing sight – like a meteor –

INSERT CUT: BORDEN SPEEDS THROUGH THE NIGHT . . .

BORDEN
(V.O.)
A V-2 rocket heading for England –

INSERT CUT: A ROCKET STREAKS PAST, RIPPING APART THE DARK . . .

BORDEN
(V.O.)
I can't help but imagine what it will be for such an enemy rocket to carry an *atomic* warhead . . .

INSERT CUT: A MISSILE RISES THROUGH THE CLOUDS . . .

I hear the sound of FEET STAMPING . . .

INSERT CUT: DOZENS OF FEET STAMPING FASTER AND FASTER . . .

I peer into the future . . .

INSERT CUT: HUNDREDS OF MISSILES RISE THROUGH THE CLOUDS . . .

I look at the map . . . Rabi's circles EXPAND like raindrops in a puddle . . .

OPPENHEIMER
Then let's make sure we're not the ones to make that possible.

But that's not the answer Borden wanted. He leaves. Fermi and Bush remain. Rabi leans over to me.

RABI
Oppie, you don't want to go up against Strauss.

OPPENHEIMER

If we both speak, they listen to me.

RABI

When you speak, they hear a prophet. When Strauss speaks, they hear themselves.

OPPENHEIMER

They'll listen to a prophet.

RABI

A prophet can't be wrong. Not once.

SENATOR McGEE
(V.O.)

Didn't you accuse Oppenheimer of sabotaging the development of the Super?

Cut to:

INT. SENATE COMMITTEE HEARING ROOM – DAY (B&W)

Strauss shifts uneasily in his chair.

STRAUSS

I was never one of those who bandied around terms like 'sabotage'.

SENATOR McGEE

But Mr Borden was?

STRAUSS

As I understand it.

SENATOR McGEE

How was Mr Borden able to put together such a detailed indictment? He was no longer a government employee, and yet he appears to have had unlimited access to Dr Oppenheimer's file. Might Mr Nichols have given him access to the file? Or someone else at the AEC?

>STRAUSS

Feelings ran high on these issues, but that's a very serious accusation, Senator.

Cut to:

EXT. LOS ALAMOS – DAY (COLOUR)

RAIN. I ride my horse through the outskirts. Spot a FLIER stapled to a telegraph pole, ink running: 'THE IMPACT OF THE GADGET ON CIVILIZATION – DISCUSSION, BLDG T31 SUNDAY, 11AM'.

INT. CYCLOTRON BUILDING, LOS ALAMOS – DAY

I enter to find forty scientists meeting. Hornig is speaking.

>HORNIG
Germany's about to surrender, the Japanese are losing. It's no longer the enemy who are the greatest threat to mankind – it's us. Our work.

Heads turn as they notice me.

>OPPENHEIMER
Hitler's dead. But the Japanese fight on.

The audience is now turned my way . . .

>HORNIG
Their defeat seems assured.

>OPPENHEIMER
Not if you're a GI preparing to invade Japan. We can end this war.

>MORRISON
How can we justify using this weapon on human beings?

>OPPENHEIMER
We're theorists – we can imagine a future, and our imaginings horrify us. But they won't fear it until they

understand it, and they won't understand it until they've used it. When the world learns the terrible secret of Los Alamos, our work will ensure a peace mankind has never seen. A peace based on the kind of international cooperation that Roosevelt always envisaged.

Some of the scientists nod. Scattered applause . . .

INSERT CUT: THE GOLDFISH BOWL IS FULL OF MARBLES . . .

EXT. LOS ALAMOS – DAY

I walk down the main drag with Groves.

> OPPENHEIMER
>
> Progress.

> GROVES
>
> Two years and a billion dollars' worth?

> OPPENHEIMER
>
> Hard to put a price on it.

> GROVES
>
> Not really. Just add up the bills.
> (points)
> 'Rural free delivery' . . . Eighty babies delivered the first year. This year they've had ten a month.

> OPPENHEIMER
>
> Birth control's a little out of my jurisdiction, General.

Groves watches Kitty approach – she's HEAVILY PREGNANT.

> GROVES
>
> Clearly.

EXT. CANYON, LOS ALAMOS – DAY

An IMPLOSION DEVICE ROCKS the canyon. Groves, Fuchs and I raise our heads – Kistiakowsky and Hornig rush to the device –

KISTIAKOWSKY

    That's the one!

I put my PIPE on the wall as we CLIMB out of the bunker . . .

GROVES

    Two viable bombs. I need a date.

OPPENHEIMER

    September –

GROVES

    July –

Kistiakowsky waves a trail of ticker tape –

KISTIAKOWSKY

    That's the sweet spot, gentlemen!

OPPENHEIMER

    August.

GROVES

    July –

OPPENHEIMER

    A test in July.

Fuchs hands me my pipe. I dust it off . . .

OPPENHEIMER

    But I need my brother.
                (off his look)
    Frank knows the desert. He left politics behind – he's been
    working for Lawrence for two years.

INSERT CUT: FLYING OVER DESERT TO FIND FRANK STANDING BY
A JEEP WITH AN ARMY OFFICER.

GROVES

    What do we call the test?

OPPENHEIMER
             (thinking)
    'Batter my heart, three-person'd god.'

                          GROVES
  What?

                       OPPENHEIMER
  Trinity.

INSERT CUT: A STEEL TOWER IS RAISED IN THE DESERT . . .

INT. ROOM 2022, ATOMIC ENERGY COMMISSION –
DAY

                           ROBB
  So you insisted on bringing on your brother, Frank, a
  known Communist –

                       OPPENHEIMER
  Former Communist –

                           ROBB
  You brought a known *former* Communist onto America's
  most secret and important defence project?

                       OPPENHEIMER
  I knew my brother could be trusted absolutely.

                           ROBB
  And you feel your judgement was sound on who on the
  team could be trusted?

                      KISTIAKOWSKY
                          (O.S.)
  Fuchs! Head down!

EXT. BERM – DAY

Behind a berm, Groves, Fuchs, Frank and I watch Kistiakowsky
and Hornig arm a detonator. Fuchs shuffles lower.

                      KISTIAKOWSKY
  Everybody ready . . .?

Kistiakowsky triggers A VAST EXPLOSION, SPLINTERING THE TOWER, SENDING A MASSIVE PLUME OF FIRE INTO THE AIR . . . the SHOCKWAVE throws DEBRIS onto me and Groves . . .

> GROVES
> I hope you learned something.

> FRANK
> We learned we're gonna need to be *a lot* further away . . .

> GROVES
> Well, figure it out. Fast.
> (to me)
> We leave for Washington tomorrow, and we're going to give them a date.

INT. HOTEL LOBBY, WASHINGTON, DC – DAY

I walk across the lobby – someone GRABS my arm – Szilard, with the Scientist with Glasses in tow. I glance out the window, where Groves is getting into a car, waiting for me . . .

> OPPENHEIMER
> You're a long way from Chicago, Leo.

> SZILARD
> If we don't act now, they're going to use this thing against Japan. We booked a meeting with Truman, but somebody killed it. You're meeting the Secretary of War –

> OPPENHEIMER
> Just because we're building it doesn't mean we get to decide how it's used.

> SZILARD
> History will judge us, Robert. In Chicago we put together a petition –

Glasses holds out a paper – I PUSH it back – Glasses FLINCHES –

OPPENHEIMER

I'm not getting into that. Tell me your concerns and I'll relay them –

SZILARD

My *concerns*?! Germany's defeated, Japan's not going to hold out alone –

OPPENHEIMER

How would you know? You got us into this, you and Einstein, with your letter to Roosevelt saying we could build a bomb –

SZILARD

Against *Germany*.

OPPENHEIMER

That's not how weapons manufacture works, Szilard.

SZILARD

Oppie, you have to help.

OPPENHEIMER

Fermi's in the meeting. And Lawrence –

SZILARD

They're not *you*. You're the great salesman of science – you can convince anyone of anything. Even yourself.

INT. SECRETARY OF WAR'S OFFICE – DAY

I sit on a couch next to Fermi – Lawrence, Groves and Bush in chairs. Secretary of War STIMSON presides. Military, scientists and officials are scattered through the room.

STIMSON

The firestorm in Tokyo killed one hundred thousand people. Mostly civilians. I worry about an America where we do these things and no one protests.

131

MARSHALL

Pearl Harbor and three years of brutal conflict in the
Pacific buys a lot of latitude with the American public.

STIMSON

Enough to unleash the atomic bomb?

FERMI

In truth, the A-bomb might not cause as much damage as
the Tokyo bombings.

STIMSON

What are we estimating?

BUSH

In a medium-sized city, twenty or thirty thousand dead.

OPPENHEIMER

Don't underestimate the psychological impact of an atomic
explosion . . . a pillar of fire ten thousand feet tall, deadly
neutron effects for a mile in all directions . . . from one.
Single. Device. Dropped from a barely noticed B-29 . . . the
atomic bomb will be a terrible revelation of divine power.

Groves carefully monitors my effect on the room . . .

MARSHALL

If that's true it would be definitive. World War II would be
over. Our boys would come home.

STIMSON

This could end the war.

OPPENHEIMER

This could end *all* war. If we retain moral advantage.

Groves registers the pivot . . .

STIMSON

How so?

OPPENHEIMER

If we use this weapon without informing our allies, they'll
see it as a threat and we'll be in an arms race.

MARSHALL

How open can we be with the Soviets?

BUSH

Secrecy won't stop the Soviets becoming part of the atomic world.

A politician, BYRNES, clears his throat politely –

BYRNES

We've been told they have no uranium.

BUSH

You've been misinformed. A Russian bomb is a matter of time.

LAWRENCE

To stay ahead, our programme has to continue at full pace after the war.

OPPENHEIMER

Secretary Stimson, if I may. Not all the scientists on the project agree. In fact, this might be a moment to consider other opinions –

GROVES

The Manhattan Project's been plagued from the start by certain scientists of doubtful discretion and uncertain loyalty. One of them just tried to get a meeting with the President.

I say nothing. Groves looks directly at me.

GROVES

We need them for now, but as soon as is practical, we should sever any such scientists from the programme. Wouldn't you agree, doctor?

I meet Groves' gaze. Stay silent . . . Nod.

MARSHALL

If a Russian bomb is inevitable, perhaps we should invite their top scientists to Trinity.

BYRNES

President Truman has no intention of raising expectations
that Stalin be included in the atomic project.

STIMSON

Informing him of our breakthrough, and presenting it
as the means to win the war need not make unkeepable
promises. But the Potsdam peace conference in July is the
last chance for Truman to have that conversation. Can you
give us a working bomb by then?

GROVES

Absolutely. We'll test-fire before the conference.

STIMSON

And Japan?

OPPENHEIMER

If the test works you'll have two bombs for August.

STIMSON

Military targets?

OPPENHEIMER

There aren't any big enough.

CONANT

Perhaps a vital war plant, with workers housed nearby.

FERMI

Could we issue a warning? To reduce civilian casualties.

AIR FORCE OFFICER

They'd send up everything they have against us, and I'd be
in that plane.

BUSH

If we announce it and it fails to go off we'd scupper any
chance of Japanese surrender.

LAWRENCE

Is there no way to demonstrate the bomb to Japan to
provoke surrender?

GROVES

We intend to demonstrate it in the most unambiguous
terms. Twice. Once to show the weapon's power. A second
to show that we can keep going until they surrender.

STIMSON

We have a list of twelve cities to choose from. Sorry,
eleven, I've taken Kyoto off the list because of its cultural
significance to the Japanese people.

Stimson senses the unease in the room . . .

STIMSON

Let me make this simple for you, gentlemen. The Japanese
will not surrender short of a successful invasion of the
home islands. Many lives, American and Japanese, will be
lost in that invasion. The use of the atomic bomb against
Japanese cities will save lives.

EXT. BASE OF STEEL TOWER, TRINITY TEST SITE – DAY

Frank shows Groves and me the site plan . . .

FRANK

Ground Zero. Observation posts at ten thousand yards
north, south and west.

OPPENHEIMER

Where do we trigger from?

FRANK

South ten thousand. Base camp is ten miles south, here.
And a further observation point on this hill twenty miles
away.

I point to a crew digging a trench from the base of the tower.

OPPENHEIMER

What's that? The trigger lines went in already.

FRANK

The air force requested a line of lights for their B-29.

OPPENHEIMER

What B-29? Our bomb's on the tower.

FRANK

They want to use the test to confirm the safe operating
distance.

GROVES

Risky.

FRANK

Not as risky as dropping one over Japan and hoping we
were right about the blast radius.

OPPENHEIMER

Don't let them slow us down – we're firing on the 15th.

FRANK

The 15th?! That's not –

Frank sees my expression –

FRANK

The 15th.

INT. LECTURE HALL, T-SECTION, LOS ALAMOS – DAY

I show the plan to the division heads.

OPPENHEIMER

I'll be at the south observation point with Frank and
Kistiakowsky. You'll all be assigned to base camp, far
observation, or west observation.

INSERT CUT: I ENTER A TENT AT THE BASE OF THE TOWER – THE
SILVER SPHERE OF THE BOMB IS SURROUNDED BY THE TEAM . . .

BETHE

Are those safe distances?

OPPENHEIMER

They're based on your calculations.

RABI
Time to stand behind your science, Hans. Literally.

INSERT CUT: THE BOMB IS HOISTED UP INTO THE TOWER . . .

TELLER
What about the radiation cloud?

OPPENHEIMER
Without high winds it should settle within two to three miles. Evacuation measures will be in place, but we need good weather for visibility so it should be fine. We go on the night of the 15th.

The team exchange looks –

OPPENHEIMER
That's a hard deadline, so if anyone has anything . . . speak now.

BETHE
We need a final implosion test.

KISTIAKOWSKY
Couldn't hurt.

OPPENHEIMER
Do it. Is there anything else that might stop us?

A THUNDERCLAP takes us into –

EXT. OPPENHEIMER HOUSE, LOS ALAMOS – DAY

White sheets FLAP CRAZILY in the wind . . . through the window we see Kitty put her drink down reluctantly. She comes out to grab a sheet that has come loose from the line . . . notices a JEEP idling at the gate, ARMED GUARDS patiently waiting . . .

I emerge from the house carrying an overnight bag. Kitty, one hand on the washing line, turns to look at me, curious.

KITTY
It's happening, isn't it?

137

I watch the sheets flapping. Glance at the guards . . .

>   OPPENHEIMER
> I'll send a message. If it's gone our way . . . 'Take in the
> sheets.'

She nods. I head towards the waiting jeep.

>   KITTY
> Robert?

I turn, looking at Kitty amongst the FLAPPING SHEETS . . .

>   KITTY
> Break a leg.

EXT. CANYON, LOS ALAMOS – DAY

A BANG as the final implosion test goes off . . . Kistiakowsky
and Fuchs raise their heads . . . Kistiakowsky shows Fuchs the
tape, grave.

EXT. STEEL TOWER, TRINITY TEST SITE – EVENING

I watch the last TECHNICIAN come down. I nod at the man, then
starts my lonely climb . . .

I stare at the silver sphere of the first atomic bomb, its surface
STUDDED with detonators, WIRES DRAPED across it like
spaghetti. Thunder RUMBLES. I watch the approaching storm . . .

EXT. BASE CAMP, TRINITY TEST SITE – EVENING

Army tents. A WINDMILL SPINS FURIOUSLY . . .

INT. BASE CAMP, TRINITY TEST SITE – EVENING

Fermi moves through the team, taking bets . . .

FERMI

Oppie's taken a very modest three kilotons . . . Teller's in
for forty-five . . .

Rabi pulls out some bills –

RABI

Twenty.

FERMI

Twenty thousand tons of TNT . . . and does anyone want
the side action on total atmospheric ignition?

The scientists groan and laugh. Soldiers look at each other:
'What the hell?' Groves corners the army WEATHERMAN.

GROVES

Are you saying we'll have to delay?

WEATHERMAN

I'm saying it would be prudent.

OPPENHEIMER

Has this weather reached the site?

The weatherman gets on his radio. Kistiakowsky BURSTS in –

KISTIAKOWSKY

Oppie –

The phone rings –

KISTIAKOWSKY

Bethe's calling you to tell you the implosion test failed,
but –

I have the phone to my ear –

OPPENHEIMER

Hans. Yes, he's here. Yes.
            (I hang up)
Is he wrong?

KISTIAKOWSKY

No.

OPPENHEIMER
So we're about to fire a dud?

KISTIAKOWSKY
No.

GROVES
Explain.

KISTIAKOWSKY
I can't. I just know the implosion lenses will work.

OPPENHEIMER
If we fire those detonators and they don't trigger the reaction, two years' worth of plutonium will be scattered across white sands.

KISTIAKOWSKY
(holds out his hand)
A month of my salary against ten bucks says it lights.

I study Kistiakowsky. Take the bet.

WEATHERMAN
The wind's picking up at Zero, not the rain. Lightning circling.

THUNDER. Rabi calls over –

RABI
Hey, weatherman, you think it might be time to get your men away from the steel tower with the atomic bomb primed to detonate via electrical charge?

The weatherman laughs. Then GRABS the radio –

WEATHERMAN
Pull 'em out.

OPPENHEIMER
(to Groves)
Let's get to south observation. Make our determination there.

EXT. STEEL TOWER, TRINITY TEST SITE – NIGHT

The last trucks drive away, lightning on the horizon. The bomb sits there, impervious to peals of DRY THUNDER . . .

EXT. SOUTH OBSERVATION POST, TRINITY TEST SITE – NIGHT

Groves, the weatherman and I watch rain LASH the desert . . .

                    OPPENHEIMER
The team hasn't slept for two nights. We stand down, make the bomb safe, it's weeks before we get back here.

                    GROVES
Then we miss Potsdam.
                    (checks watch)
I need to get word to Truman by seven.
                    (to the weatherman)
Our window's closing. What's it doing?

                    WEATHERMAN
Raining. Blowing. Lightning.

                    GROVES
For how long, dammit?!

                    WEATHERMAN
It's holding strong.

                    OPPENHEIMER
It'll break before dawn.

                    GROVES
How could you know that?

                    OPPENHEIMER
I know this desert. The air cools overnight. Just before dawn, the storm breaks.

                    WEATHERMAN
He could be right. But schedule it as late as possible.

OPPENHEIMER

Five thirty?

Groves considers this. Turns to the weatherman.

GROVES

Sign your forecast. If you're wrong, I'll hang you.

INT. BUNKER, SOUTH OBSERVATION POST – NIGHT

Groves and me, alone. Rain pelting down outside.

GROVES

Three years. Four thousand people. Two billion dollars. If it doesn't go off we're both finished.

OPPENHEIMER

I put my money on three kilotons. Any less, they won't get what it is.

GROVES

What did Fermi mean by 'atmospheric ignition'?

OPPENHEIMER

We had a moment where it looked like the chain reaction from an atomic device might never stop. Setting fire to the atmosphere.

GROVES

Why's Fermi still taking side bets on it?

OPPENHEIMER

Call it gallows humour.

Groves takes this in. Picks the scab –

GROVES

Are we saying there's a chance that when we push that button . . . we destroy the world?

OPPENHEIMER

Nothing in our research over the last three years supports that conclusion except as the most remote possibility.

                    GROVES
How remote?

                  OPPENHEIMER
The chances are near zero.

                    GROVES
Near zero?

                  OPPENHEIMER
                   (smiling)
What do you want from theory alone?

                    GROVES
Zero would be nice.

I check my watch.

                  OPPENHEIMER
Well, in an hour and fifty-eight minutes, we'll know.

I listen –

                  OPPENHEIMER
It's letting up . . .

EXT. TRINITY TEST SITE – NIGHT

Searchlights settle on the gleaming steel tower. A line of lights
leading from the the blackness of the night-time desert to the
tower comes on . . .

EXT. SOUTH OBSERVATION POST, TRINITY TEST SITE –
CONTINUOUS

Groves and I come out into gentle rain. The wind has fallen off.
Frank comes up to meet us.

                    FRANK
The arming party's left Zero, heading this way, throwing
the switches . . .

(to the soldiers)
Turn the cars, ready for emergency evacuation . . .

EXT. SOUTH 1500 POST – NIGHT

Kistiakowsky and military personal, including BAINBRIDGE,
get out of a truck. Kistiakowsky THROWS a SWITCH on the
ground . . .

EXT. BASE CAMP, TRINITY TEST SITE – CONTINUOUS

Rabi, Fermi and Bethe come outside. A SOLDIER hands them
WELDER'S GLASS . . .

EXT. SOUTH OBSERVATION POST, TRINITY TEST SITE –
NIGHT

Kistiakowsky and Bainbridge get out of the truck and enter the
bunker.

INT. SOUTH OBSERVATION POST, TRINITY TEST SITE –
CONTINUOUS

Bainbridge pulls out a key. UNLOCKS the arming switches.
Kistiakowsky nods, Bainbridge THROWS THE SWITCHES.

BAINBRIDGE

Twenty minutes.

EXT. TRINITY TEST SITE – CONTINUOUS

A SIGNAL ROCKET flares up into the air . . .

EXT. BASE CAMP, TRINITY TEST SITE – CONTINUOUS

Rabi, Fermi and the others watch the rocket go up –

FERMI

Twenty minutes!

EXT. HILLTOP DISTANT OBSERVATION POINT –
CONTINUOUS

A group of scientists, including Teller, Feynman and Lawrence, watch the distant rocket sputter . . .

FEYNMAN
That's twenty!

DARK GLASSES are handed out. Feynman refuses, jumping up into the cab of a truck –

SOLDIER
Hey, Feynman –

Feynman TAPS the windshield –

FEYNMAN
The glass stops the UV.

Teller, in dark glasses, is APPLYING SUNSCREEN at night –

TELLER
But what stops the glass?

Feynman looks at Teller. Looks at the glass, shakes his head, grinning . . .

INT. SOUTH OBSERVATION POST, TRINITY TEST SITE –
CONTINUOUS

Groves moves to me –

GROVES
I'm heading to base camp. Best of luck.

Groves shakes my hand.

GROVES
Try not to blow up the world.

INT. SAME – MOMENTS LATER

I watch Bainbridge take his place at the KILL SWITCH.

OPPENHEIMER
Watch that needle. If the detonators don't charge, or if the voltage dips below one volt, you abort.

Bainbridge nods, watching the meter of the X-unit like a hawk. A nervous hawk.

EXT. BASE CAMP, TRINITY TEST SITE – CONTINUOUS

A loudspeaker broadcasts the countdown –

LOUDSPEAKER
Two minutes to detonation . . .

The two-minute rocket goes up –

ARMY CAPTAIN
Everybody down!

The observers lie on the ground, facing away from the site.

ARMY CAPTAIN
Do not turn around until you see light reflected on the hills. Then look at the explosion only through the welder's glass . . .

LOUDSPEAKER
Ninety seconds . . .

EXT. DISTANT OBSERVATION POINT – CONTINUOUS

Feynman TUNES the radio into the countdown relay –

RADIO
Sixty seconds . . .

Lawrence jumps in next to Feynman. The scientists peer into the distance through the windshield . . . Teller, pale with sunscreen, adjusts his dark glasses . . .

INT. SOUTH OBSERVATION POST, TRINITY TEST SITE —
CONTINUOUS

Bainbridge PEERS at the X-unit . . . Frank and I peer at the
tower . . . The electronic counter STARTS: 45, 44, 43, 42 . . .

> OPPENHEIMER
> These things are hard on your heart.

> LOUDSPEAKER
> Thirty seconds . . .

FOUR RED LIGHTS flicker on –

EXT. STEEL TOWER, TRINITY TEST SITE — CONTINUOUS

The bomb WAKES, detonators on its surface HUMMING . . .

INT. SOUTH OBSERVATION POST, TRINITY TEST SITE —
CONTINUOUS

The NEEDLE on the X-unit SHOOTS to the right –

> BAINBRIDGE
> Detonators charged!

I pull on a pair of WELDER'S GOGGLES . . .

EXT. BASE CAMP, TRINITY TEST SITE — CONTINUOUS

Rabi lifts his head to peek around, welder's glass over his
eyes . . . Groves shakes hands with Bush . . .

> LOUDSPEAKER
> . . . eighteen, seventeen . . .

EXT. DISTANT OBSERVATION POINT — CONTINUOUS

Feynman peers through the windshield. Teller studies the
horizon . . .

. . . twelve, eleven . . .

INT. SOUTH OBSERVATION POST, TRINITY TEST SITE –
CONTINUOUS

A GONG sounds at T-minus 10 – Bainbridge peers at the needle,
which BOBBLES – his hand FLINCHES – the needle settles . . .

LOUDSPEAKER
Ten, nine, eight . . .

Frank and I peer through the holes in the concrete.

LOUDSPEAKER
. . . seven, six, five . . .

Kistiakowsky SCRAMBLES out of the bunker –

EXT. SOUTH OBSERVATION POST, TRINITY TEST SITE –
CONTINUOUS

– and up onto the embankment, eyes locked on the tiny glow of
the distant tower . . .

LOUDSPEAKER
. . . four, three . . .

INT. SOUTH OBSERVATION POST, TRINITY TEST SITE –
CONTINUOUS

I stare straight ahead . . .

LOUDSPEAKER
. . . two, one . . .

Bainbridge watches the needle as the counter goes down to –

. . . zero.

My breath stops – an agonizing instant before – SILENT LIGHT.
FULL BRIGHT NOON SUNNY DAYLIGHT.

EXT. BASE CAMP, TRINITY TEST SITE – CONTINUOUS

Rabi sees SUDDEN DAYTIME – turns to the LIGHT, peers through the welder's glass at BLINDING SILENT WHITE . . .

EXT. DISTANT OBSERVATION POINT – CONTINUOUS

Lawrence is stepping out of the car as Feynman SHUTS his eyes against INSTANT DAYLIGHT . . . a HUSHED INTAKE OF BREATH from the crowd of sunglasses-clad distant observers . . .

INT. SOUTH OBSERVATION POST, TRINITY TEST SITE – CONTINUOUS

All we can hear is my TREMULOUS BREATHING as the LIGHT becomes less BLINDING, resolving into a FIREBALL, BRIGHT AS THE SUN, BUT GIANT . . . I YANK off my goggles . . . watch the ROILING PLASMA become more visible in its HELLISH CONTORTIONS . . . CLIMBING into the sky like the DEVIL'S CLAW . . .

My PUPILS are PINPRICKS –

OPPENHEIMER
(V.O.)
Now I am become Death, destroyer of worlds . . .

And then – CRACK!! . . . !!! . . . !!!! . . . !!!!! . . .

I am hit by the WIND and DUST of the SHOCKWAVE –

THE THUNDER OF A THOUSAND STORMS ROLLS OVER, DEAFENING –

EXT. SOUTH OBSERVATION POST, TRINITY TEST SITE

Kistiakowsky is BLOWN OFF HIS FEET . . .

INT. SOUTH OBSERVATION POST, TRINITY TEST SITE –
CONTINUOUS

With the wave of DARK THUNDER, TERRIBLE BEAUTY GIVES
WAY TO FEAR . . . I TREMBLE as I watch the glowing cloud
climb to its full height, its inner fire dimming to a HELLISH
SCARLET . . . DUST CLOUD RISING, CRACKLING WITH PURPLISH
ENERGY . . .

As the sound diminishes to a RUMBLE and night REGAINS the
desert floor, Frank turns to me –

> FRANK
> (quiet)
>
> It worked.

I nod, awestruck . . .

EXT. BASE CAMP, TRINITY TEST SITE – CONTINUOUS

Startled murmurs, then a few claps . . . then CRAZY, CHEERING,
CLAPPING, DANCING . . . in the middle of it all Rabi tries to
understand what just happened . . .

EXT. SAME – CONTINUOUS

ECSTATIC CHEERING . . . even Teller SMILES . . . Feynman pulls
out some BONGOS and hops onto the hood of the truck . . .
people DANCE to his PAGAN RHYTHM as the dawn CREEPS IN . . .

EXT. SOUTH OBSERVATION POST, TRINITY TEST SITE –
CONTINUOUS

Kistiakowsky GRABS me in a big HUG – steps back – holding
out his hand for payment. I pull out my wallet, frown – there's
nothing in it –

> OPPENHEIMER
>
> I'm good for it.

Kistiakowsky GRINS –

>   KISTIAKOWSKY
> Yes, you are! Yes, you are!

EXT. BASE CAMP, TRINITY TEST SITE – MOMENTS
LATER

Rabi, still amidst the celebration, watches a car pull up.

I get out, walking like GARY FUCKING COOPER – the crowd spots
me . . . goes NUTS . . .

Groves turns to an AIDE –

>   GROVES
> Get me Potsdam. Right away.

I nod at Groves, move through the sea of congratulations to find
Serber . . .

>   OPPENHEIMER
> Get a message to Kitty . . .

Serber's face falls, perturbed –

>   SERBER
> We can't say anything –

>   OPPENHEIMER
> Just tell her to bring in the sheets.

Serber grins. I spot Groves on a FIELD TELEPHONE – then am
HOISTED ONTO JOYFUL SHOULDERS . . .

INT. OPPENHEIMER HOUSE, LOS ALAMOS – DAY

Kitty wrangles the kitchen phone while she feeds our baby
daughter and young son –

>   KITTY
> Sorry. Yes, Charlotte, go ahead.

> CHARLOTTE
> (over phone)
Well, I don't know, he just said to tell you to bring in the sheets.

Kitty freezes, letting the phone come off her ear . . .

> CHARLOTTE
> (over phone)
Kitty? Kitty?

Kitty smiles, tears forming. It is done.

Fade out.

Fade in:

EXT. T-SECTION, LOS ALAMOS – DAY

I watch CRATES hoisted on trucks by the army . . .

> OPPENHEIMER
> (V.O.)
They musn't drop it through cloud cover –

INT. T-SECTION, LOS ALAMOS – DAY

I am talking to the AIR FORCE OFFICER who is supervising the crating of equipment –

> OPPENHEIMER
If they detonate it too high in the air, the blast won't be as powerful –

> AIR FORCE OFFICER
With respect, Dr Oppenheimer. We'll take it from here.

I lose sight of the bomb as THE CRATE IS CLOSED.

EXT. T-SECTION, LOS ALAMOS – DAY

Groves appears at my side, watching the loading . . .

OPPENHEIMER

Did Truman brief Stalin at Potsdam?

GROVES

'Brief' would be an overstatement. He referred to a
powerful new weapon, Stalin said he hoped we'd make
good use of it against Japan.

OPPENHEIMER

That's it?

GROVES

Robert, we've given them an ace. It's for them to play the
hand.

Frustrated, I drop my cigarette and GRIND it out –

OPPENHEIMER

You're aiming for the 6th?

GROVES

That's up to the CO in the Pacific.

OPPENHEIMER

Should I come with you to Washington?

GROVES

What for?

OPPENHEIMER

Well . . . you'll keep me informed?

Groves turns to leave –

GROVES

Of course.
(looks back)
As best I can.

I watch Groves leave, uneasy. A truck pulls out, REVEALING
TELLER. He crosses, watching the loaded truck move away . . .

TELLER

Would the Japanese surrender if they knew what was
coming?

OPPENHEIMER

I don't know.

TELLER

Have you seen Szilard's petition?

OPPENHEIMER

Yeah. What the hell does Szilard know about the Japanese?

I look at Teller.

OPPENHEIMER

You're not signing it?

TELLER

A lot of people have.

OPPENHEIMER

Edward, the fact that we built this bomb doesn't give us
any more right or responsibility to decide how it's used
than anyone else.

TELLER

But we're the only people who know about it.

OPPENHEIMER

I've told Stimson the various opinions of the community.

TELLER

But what's *your* opinion?

I watch another truck pull out . . .

OPPENHEIMER

Once it's used, nuclear war, maybe all war, becomes
unthinkable.

TELLER

Until somebody builds a bigger bomb.

INT. OPPENHEIMER HOUSE, LOS ALAMOS – NIGHT

Kitty comes downstairs to find me sitting at the kitchen table.
The phone in front of me.

> OPPENHEIMER
> I thought they would call.

> KITTY
> It's only the 5th.

> OPPENHEIMER
> In Japan it's the 6th.

INT. OPPENHEIMER'S OFFICE, LOS ALAMOS – DAY

I pace my office, agitated.

> OPPENHEIMER
> Charlotte? Try Groves again.

> CHARLOTTE
> (O.S.)
> Truman's on the Radio –!

I BOLT into –

INT. FOYER, OPPENHEIMER'S OFFICE – CONTINUOUS

Charlotte is patching the PA to the radio –

> TRUMAN
> (over radio)
> . . . Sixteen hours ago an American airplane dropped one
> bomb on Hiroshima and destroyed its usefulness to the
> enemy . . .

INT. OFFICE, T-SECTION, LOS ALAMOS – DAY

Frank is doing paperwork when the PA WHISTLES –

> TRUMAN
> (over PA)
> That bomb had more power than twenty thousand tons of
> TNT . . .

INT. CORRIDOR, T-SECTION, LOS ALAMOS –
CONTINUOUS

As Frank emerges, others DRIFT into the corridor, shocked . . .

> TRUMAN
> (over PA)
> It is an atomic bomb. It is a harnessing of the basic power
> of the universe . . .

He hears BANGING and CHEERING – through the window
SOLDIERS BEAT on trash-can lids. Frank and the scientists try
uncertain smiles and handshakes . . .

INT. OPPENHEIMER'S OFFICE, LOS ALAMOS – DAY

I listen to the radio –

> TRUMAN
> (over radio)
> The force from which the sun draws its power has been
> loosed against those who brought war to the Far East . . .

> CHARLOTTE
> (O.S.)
> Groves on one!

I white-knuckle the phone . . .

> GROVES
> (over phone)
> I'm very proud of you and all of your people.

> OPPENHEIMER
> It went alright?

GROVES
(over phone)
Apparently it went with a tremendous bang.

OPPENHEIMER
Everybody here is feeling reasonably good about it. It's
been a long road.

GROVES
(over phone)
I think one of the wisest things I ever did was when
I selected the director of Los Alamos.

I gently put down the phone . . .

TRUMAN
(over radio)
We have spent two billion dollars . . .

EXT. LOS ALAMOS – CONTINUOUS

I walk in a relieved daze . . .

TRUMAN
(over radio)
. . . on the greatest scientific gamble in history and won.

Horns HONK, soldiers CHEER . . . people WAVE . . . I nod
back . . .

INT. FULLER LODGE, LOS ALAMOS – NIGHT

A restless, excitable CROWD is packed into the bleachers, like a
HIGH-SCHOOL PEP RALLY . . .

INT. LOBBY, FULLER LODGE, LOS ALAMOS –
CONTINUOUS

Kitty reaches forward and adjusts my tie. We hear the sound of
DOZENS OF FEET STAMPING RHYTHMICALLY . . .

INT. FULLER LODGE, LOS ALAMOS – CONTINUOUS

The impatient crowd is STAMPING IN UNISON . . .

INT. LOBBY, FULLER LODGE, LOS ALAMOS –
CONTINUOUS

Kitty nods at me, I take a breath and PUSH through the door –

INT. FULLER LODGE, LOS ALAMOS – CONTINUOUS

As I walk past the rear bleachers I get a close view of DOZENS
OF FEET STAMPING IN UNISON . . . the STAMPING FEET GET
FASTER as I approach the stage . . .

The STAMPING GROWS OPPRESSIVE – FASTER and FASTER until
RHYTHM BREAKS, causing CACOPHONY which PEAKS as I step
up . . .

I raise my hands in a theatrically victorious gesture – the crowd
CHEERS . . .

> OPPENHEIMER
> The world will remember this day.

LOUDER CHEERING . . .

> OPPENHEIMER
> It's too early to determine what the results of the bombing
> are . . .

Though the crowd is still CHEERING, their sound DIMINISHES . . .

> OPPENHEIMER
> But I'm sure the Japanese didn't like it –

CHEERS. CHEERS. CHEERS. BUT NO SOUND. As I look out at the
EXCITED FACES I can hear my own BREATHING . . . I carry on –

> OPPENHEIMER
> I'm proud of what you accomplished . . .

The crowd seems to go NUTS, but all we hear is the QUIET
CREAKING OF SEATS and SHUFFLE OF FEET as they REACT, HANDS
SILENTLY CLAPPING, MOUTHS SILENTLY JAWING . . . I try again –

                    OPPENHEIMER
     I just wish we'd had it in time to use against the
     Germans . . .

The CHEERING AND CLAPPING PEOPLE GET TO THEIR FEET in
MORTIFYING SILENCE . . .

I stare at them, straining to hear something, then –

PIERCING SCREAMS not cheers, as INSTANT DAYLIGHT
POURS IN THE WINDOWS – BRIGHTER AND BRIGHTER –

My eyes are pinpricks as I see CHEERING/SCREAMING MOUTHS
STRETCHED GROTESQUELY WIDE –

CRACK!! . . . !!! . . . !!!! . . . !!!!! . . . THE THUNDER OF A
THOUSAND STORMS ROLLS OVER, DEAFENING –

I see FLESH RIPPED FROM THE SMILING YOUNG FACES . . .
I see PLASMA ROILING and the DEVIL'S CLAW reach into the
night sky . . . I see piles of ASHES where the young crowd was
cheering . . .

INT. SAME – LATER

I DRIFT through a SILENT, KINETIC WHIRLWIND OF
CELEBRATION, CLAPPED on the back, KISSED . . . NODDING and
HOLLOW SMILES . . .

I see a YOUNG WOMAN LAUGHING . . . I STEP on something, look
down to see my foot inside a CHARRED CORPSE . . . I look up,
SHAKING OFF THE IMAGE . . . I see young people MAKING OUT
under the bleachers, a hand up a sweater . . . I see the young
woman again but NOW SHE JUST CRIES AND CRIES AND CRIES . . .

INT. LOBBY, FULLER LODGE, LOS ALAMOS –
CONTINUOUS

DRIFTING through . . . I see a young man sitting, back to the
wall, WEEPING, a woman trying to console him . . .

EXT. FULLER LODGE, LOS ALAMOS – CONTINUOUS

As I exit, REVELERS RUN PAST, JOYFUL . . . turning, I see a young
physicist at the wall, bent double . . .

As I pass, he looks up, DISTRAUGHT, VOMIT AROUND HIS
MOUTH.

Fade to black.

INT. LOBBY, OVAL OFFICE, THE WHITE HOUSE – DAY

Relief. Gentle formality. I look at the coffee table: *Time*
magazine – me on the cover: 'FATHER OF THE ATOMIC
BOMB'.

> FEMALE VOICE
> (O.S.)
> Dr Oppenheimer?

An AIDE on softly clicking heels, points at the magazine.

> AIDE
> Nice picture.

I look up at her. Blank.

> AIDE
> President Truman will see you now.

INT. OVAL OFFICE – CONTINUOUS

Truman comes from behind his desk to shake my hand –

> TRUMAN
> Dr Oppenheimer, it's an honour.

OPPENHEIMER

Mr President. Secretary Byrnes.

Byrnes nods, sits. I take a seat. Truman leans on the desk.

TRUMAN

How's it feel to be the most famous man in the world?

I can't think of an answer.

TRUMAN

You helped save a lot of American lives. What we did at Hiroshima was –

OPPENHEIMER

And Nagasaki.

TRUMAN

What?

OPPENHEIMER

Hiroshima *and* Nagasaki.

TRUMAN

Obviously. Your invention let us bring our boys home. Your country owes you a great debt.

OPPENHEIMER

It was hardly my invention.

TRUMAN

It's you on the cover of *Time*.
                    (indicates Byrnes)
Jim here tells me you're concerned about an arms race with the Soviets.

OPPENHEIMER

Well, it's that . . . now is our chance to secure international cooperation on atomic energy, and I'm concerned –

TRUMAN

You know when the Soviets are gonna have a bomb?

OPPENHEIMER

I'm not sure I could give a –

TRUMAN

Never.

I look at the President, incredulous . . .

OPPENHEIMER

Mr President, the Russians have good physicists and
abundant resources –

TRUMAN

Abundant? I don't think so.

OPPENHEIMER

They'll put everything they have . . .

I taper off.

TRUMAN

I hear you're leaving Los Alamos. What should we do with
it?

OPPENHEIMER

Give it back to the Indians.

Truman laughs. But I'm not joking. Truman looks to Byrnes for
help.

BYRNES

Dr Oppenheimer, if what you say about the Soviets is true,
we have to build up Los Alamos, not shut it down.

I WRING my hands, deeply uncomfortable . . .

OPPENHEIMER

Mr President, I feel that I have blood on my hands.

Truman looks at me differently. Pulls the crisp white
handkerchief from his breast pocket and offers it –

TRUMAN

You think anyone in Hiroshima or Nagasaki gives a shit
who built the bomb? They care who dropped it. I did.
Hiroshima isn't about *you*.

Truman gestures to Byrnes, they both RISE. I get to my feet. Awkward. As I leave I hear –

> TRUMAN
> Don't let that crybaby back in here.

The door of the Oval Office CLOSES on me . . .

> STRAUSS
> (V.O.)
> Robert saw that hand-wringing got him nowhere . . .

INT. LOBBY, OVAL OFFICE, THE WHITE HOUSE – CONTINUOUS

Walking past I notice my face staring back at me from the cover of the magazine on the table . . .

> STRAUSS
> (V.O.)
> By the time I met him, he'd fully embraced his 'father of the bomb' reputation . . .

Cut to:

INT. SENATE OFFICE – DAY (B&W)

Strauss sits talking with the Senate Aide.

> STRAUSS
> *He used his profile to influence policy . . .*

INSERT CUT: LIFE MAGAZINE – 'OPPENHEIMER, NO. 1 THINKER ON ATOMIC ENERGY' . . . OPPENHEIMER RUNS A GAUNTLET OF FLASHBULBS . . . OPPENHEIMER AND KITTY ARE PHOTOGRAPHED AT OLDEN MANOR . . .

> STRAUSS
> *But all along – with McCarthy on the rise – he knew he was vulnerable. His brother was blacklisted by every university in the country . . .*

INSERT CUT: FRANK WORKS A RANCH IN COLORADO . . .

> STRAUSS
> *Lomanitz wound up working the railroad, laying track . . .*

INSERT CUT: LOMANITZ SWINGS A HAMMER . . .

> STRAUSS
> *Chevalier went into exile . . .*

INSERT CUT: CHEVALIER CARRIES SHOPPING, STEPPING AROUND
CHICKENS IN A RURAL FRENCH ALLEY . . .

> STRAUSS
> *But none of that stopped Robert from pushing the GAC to
> recommend arms control instead of the H-bomb.*

INSERT CUT: STRAUSS MOVES THE FLOWERS ON THE TABLE IN
THE HOTEL CONFERENCE ROOM, WATCHING OPPENHEIMER . . .

> STRAUSS
> *He was devastated when that didn't go his way . . .*

INSERT CUT: HEADLINE: 'TRUMAN ANNOUNCES H-BOMB
PROGRAM' . . .

Cut to:

INT. BALLROOM, PLAZA HOTEL – NIGHT (COLOUR)

Drink in hand, I watch the room sing 'Happy Birthday' to
Strauss. Ruth Tolman is next to me, staring at the NEWSPAPER.

> RUTH
> I miss Richard more than I can bear . . .

I turn to Ruth, sympathetic.

> RUTH
> But part of me's glad he didn't live to see where this is all
> going.

I nod, understanding. She downs her drink and leaves.

                    STRAUSS
                    (O.S.)
Robert, my son and his fiancée are desperate to meet the
father of the atomic bomb . . .

Strauss is there with his adult children – I glance at them, raise
a glass, then turn away. Strauss stands there, humiliated. The
couple awkwardly moves off.

                    STRAUSS
    Is this a bad time?

                    OPPENHEIMER
What do you think, Lewis?

                    STRAUSS
I think it must have been a blow for you –

                    OPPENHEIMER
For the world.

                    STRAUSS
The world? What does Fuchs mean to rest of the world?

                    OPPENHEIMER
Fuchs? Klaus Fuchs?

Strauss looks at me with concern . . .

                    STRAUSS
You haven't heard. Klaus Fuchs, the British scientist you
put onto the implosion team at Los Alamos?

INSERT CUT: FUCHS HANDS OPPENHEIMER HIS PIPE . . .

                    STRAUSS
Turns out he was spying for the Soviets. The whole time.
I'm sorry, Robert, you must feel awful.
                    (gestures to bar)
Have another. On me.

Strauss moves off. I stand there. Frozen.

                              STRAUSS
                               (V.O.)
        After the truth about Fuchs came out, they stepped up
        surveillance on Robert. He knew his phone was tapped –

Cut to:

INT. SENATE OFFICE – DAY (B&W)
                              STRAUSS
        He was followed everywhere . . .

INSERT CUT: OPPENHEIMER, DRIVING, CHECKS HIS REAR-VIEW
MIRROR, SPOTS A SEDAN FOLLOWING HIM . . .

                              STRAUSS
        His trash picked through . . .

INSERT CUT: KITTY, FROM THE KITCHEN WINDOW, SPOTS A
SUITED MAN PICKING THROUGH THEIR TRASH . . .

                              STRAUSS
        But it never stopped him speaking his mind.

                           SENATE AIDE
        A man of conviction?

                              STRAUSS
        Sure. Or maybe he thought fame could actually <u>protect</u>
        him. When Eisenhower took over, Robert saw one more
        chance. He took it . . .

INT. CORPORATE AUDITORIUM – NIGHT (B&W)

Oppenheimer is lecturing . . . Strauss is in the crowd . . .

                           OPPENHEIMER
        America and Russia may be likened to two scorpions in
        a bottle, each capable of killing the other, but only at the
        risk of his own life. There are various aspects of this policy
        which I would like to discuss but can't. Follies that can
        occur only when even the men who know the facts can find

                               166

no one to talk about them, when the facts are too secret for discussion, and thus for thought. Candor is the only remedy. Officials in Washington have to start levelling with the American people, and telling them what the enemy already know about the atomic armaments race.

Strauss notices two generals exchanging unfavorable looks.

> STRAUSS
> (V.O.)
> A lot of scientists blame me, but how was I supposed to protect him?

INT. SENATE OFFICE – DAY (B&W)

> STRAUSS
> That was the last straw for Robert's enemies.

> SENATE AIDE
> So he had to lose his security clearance.

> STRAUSS
> And with it, his credibility.

> SENATE AIDE
> But how could they do it? He was a war hero – and he'd already told everyone about his past . . .

> STRAUSS
> Borden dredged it all up again.

> SENATE AIDE
> But how could Borden get access to Oppenheimer's FBI file? Could it have been Nichols?

> STRAUSS
> I can't imagine he'd do that. But whoever did unleashed a firestorm that burned a path from the White House right to my desk at the AEC. You see them in there trying to hang Oppenheimer round my neck. I've worked my whole life to get here – the Cabinet of the United States of America –

and now, in front of the entire country, they want to put
me back in my place . . . a lowly shoe salesman.

> COUNSEL
> *Lewis, we can win this thing.*

> SENATE AIDE
> *I think we can make the Senate grasp that you did your*
> *duty, painful though it was. Will Hill's testimony back that*
> *up?*

> COUNSEL
> *Hill should be fine.*

> STRAUSS
> *I don't really know him, but he was one of Szilard's boys in*
> *Chicago. And they never forgave Oppenheimer . . .*

Cut to:

INT. LECTURE HALL, LOS ALAMOS – NIGHT (COLOUR)

Serber and MORRISON lecture using slides we never see.

> STRAUSS
> (V.O.)
> . . . for not supporting their petition against bombing
> Japan.

I watch as part of a large audience.

> MORRISON
> This was taken thirty-one days after the bombing. Virtually
> everyone in the street for nearly a mile around was
> instantly and seriously burned by the heat of the bomb.

Serber changes the slide. I react slightly.

> MORRISON
> The hot flash burned suddenly and strangely.

SERBER

The Japanese told us of people who wore striped clothing upon whom the skin was burned in stripes.

Changes slide. I LOOK AWAY from the screen. I hear the sound of FEET STAMPING as Morrison continues . . .

MORRISON

There were many who thought themselves lucky, who crawled out of the ruins of their homes only slightly injured. But they died anyway. They died days or weeks later from the radium-like rays emitted in great numbers at the moment of the explosion.

EXT. T-SECTION, LOS ALAMOS – NIGHT

I light my pipe. Teller comes up.

TELLER

Did you read this crap in the papers? A British physicist saying the atomic bombings weren't the last act of World War II but the first act of this cold war with Russia.

OPPENHEIMER

Which physicist?

TELLER

I think you knew him. Patrick Blackett?

I remember –

INSERT CUT: BLACKETT TAKES A MOUTHFUL OF APPLE . . .

I smile to myself, rueful . . .

OPPENHEIMER

He may not be wrong. We bombed an enemy that was essentially defeated.

TELLER

Robert, you have all the influence now.

I look at Teller.

169

TELLER
Urge them to continue my research on the Super.

OPPENHEIMER
I neither can nor will, Edward.

Teller looks at me. Hurt.

TELLER
Why?

OPPENHEIMER
It's not the right use of our resources.

TELLER
Is that what you really believe?

I say nothing.

TELLER
J. Robert Oppenheimer. Sphinx-like guru of the atom.
Nobody knows what you believe. Do you?

OPPENHEIMER
(V.O.)
I hope that in years to come you will look back on your
work here with pride . . .

EXT. FULLER LODGE, LOS ALAMOS – DAY

I give my leaving address, Groves by my side. The THOUSANDS
of members of the Los Alamos community listen . . .

OPPENHEIMER
But today that pride must be tempered with a profound
concern. If atomic weapons are to be added to the arsenals
of a warring world . . . then the day will come when people
will curse the name of Los Alamos and Hiroshima. The
peoples of this world must unite or they will perish. The
atomic bomb has spelled out these words for all men to
understand.

THUNDEROUS APPLAUSE echoes around the mountains . . .

Cut to:

INT. SENATE OFFICE – MORNING (B&W)

Strauss and Counsel drink coffee. The Senate Aide BURSTS *in –*

>   SENATE AIDE
> *Sorry, Admiral – I stopped off to get this –*

The Senate Aide holds up TIME MAGAZINE: *Strauss is on the cover – 'THE STRAUSS AFFAIR, SENATE V. PRESIDENT'.*

>   SENATE AIDE
> *It seems pretty favorable . . .*

The Counsel looks over Senate Aide's shoulder –

>   COUNSEL
> *There's Oppenheimer. What's the caption?*

>   SENATE AIDE
> *'J. Robert Oppenheimer – Strauss fought him . . .*
>   *(pauses)*
> *. . . and the US won.'*

>   COUNSEL
> *That'll work.*

The Senate Aide is perturbed. Looks up at Strauss.

>   SENATE AIDE
> *Those are your words. From yesterday.*

>   STRAUSS
> *We needed to pivot.*

>   SENATE AIDE
> *But how could you know what* Time *magazine would write . . .?*

>   STRAUSS
> *Henry Luce is an old friend.*

The Senate Aide stares at Strauss, realizing . . .

SENATE AIDE
You've sat there and let me tell you how this is done. But you've been far ahead. All along . . .

STRAUSS
Survival in Washington is about knowing how to get things done.

SENATE AIDE
You get things done. What was it you said about Borden? Why get caught holding the knife yourself? I'm beginning to think that Borden was holding the knife for you.

STRAUSS
Oh?

SENATE AIDE
As Chairman of the AEC, you had access to Oppenheimer's file . . .

Cut to:

INT. ROOM 2022, ATOMIC ENERGY COMMISSION – DAY (COLOUR)

I sit there testifying. Robb checks his notes . . .

ROBB
In the years following the war, would you say you exerted a great influence on the atomic policies of the USA?

OPPENHEIMER
I think 'great' would be an overstatement.

ROBB
Really? If we look at the issue of isotopes . . . were you not personally responsible for destroying all opposition to their export?

I think back to my congressional testimony . . .

INT. CONGRESSIONAL HEARING ROOM – DAY

The room is all chuckles and smiles at my performance . . .

> OPPENHEIMER
> You can use a bottle of beer for making atomic weapons,
> in fact, you do . . . I'd say isotopes are less useful for
> atomic energy than electronic components, but more useful
> than a sandwich. I'd put them somewhere in between.

The room LAUGHS appreciatively. I lean over to Volpe –

> OPPENHEIMER
> How'd I do?

Volpe glances back at Lewis Strauss, eyes down, ENRAGED . . .

> VOLPE
> Maybe a little too well, Robert.

INT. ROOM 2022, ATOMIC ENERGY COMMISSION –
DAY

> OPPENHEIMER
> I was the spokesman, but the opinion was unanimous
> amongst scientists.

> GRAY
> That will do for today. We'll reconvene tomorrow, when
> we'll hear from Dr Isidor Rabi.

INT. HOTEL ROOM, WASHINGTON, DC – NIGHT

I sit on the bed, Garrison and his team go over notes. Kitty raids
the mini-bar.

> GARRISON
> Rabi will help us. But it's going to come down to how
> much influence Borden has been able to exert on Teller –

Kitty is laughing as she opens a miniature with her teeth.

GARRISON

Did I say something funny?

KITTY

Borden, Borden, Borden. We all know it's Strauss.

OPPENHEIMER

Kitty, Lewis brought me to Princeton.

KITTY

And you humiliated him in front of Congress.

OPPENHEIMER

That was six years ago.

KITTY

The truly vindictive are as patient as saints.

GARRISON

Strauss claims to be neutral.

Kitty THROWS the miniature at me – it SMASHES into the wall –

KITTY

Wake up! It's always been Strauss – and you know it. Why won't you fight him, for Christ's sake?!

She stalks into the bathroom, SLAMMING the door. Garrison watches me clean up the miniature . . .

GARRISON

I've said it before, Robert. We should not put her on the stand –

Cut to:

INT. SENATE OFFICE – MORNING (B & W)

The Senate Aide stares at Strauss in morbid fascination . . .

SENATE AIDE

It wasn't Nichols or Hoover or one of Truman's guys – it was you. You gave the file to Borden . . . you set him on Oppenheimer, convinced him to –

STRAUSS

Borden didn't take any convincing . . .

INT. NICHOLS' OFFICE, ATOMIC ENERGY
COMMISSION – NIGHT (B&W)

*Nichols is behind the desk, but Strauss commands the room,
instructing Borden . . .*

STRAUSS

*Take your time, use the entire file. Write up your
conclusions and send them to the FBI.*

BORDEN

The material's extensive – but it isn't new.

STRAUSS

Your conclusions will be. And they'll have to be answered.

NICHOLS

Hoover passes them to McCarthy?

STRAUSS
(shakes head)
*Oppenheimer's too slippery for that self-promoting clown.
I've talked it over with Hoover – he'll hold McCarthy at
bay while you do this at the AEC.*

NICHOLS

A trial?

STRAUSS

*No trial. You can't give Oppenheimer a platform, you
can't martyr him. We need a systematic destruction of
Oppenheimer's credibility so he can never again speak on
matters of national security.*

BORDEN

What, then?

STRAUSS

A shabby little room, far from the limelight . . .

INSERT CUT: ROOM 2022 IS OPENED UP. DUSTED, TABLES
ARRANGED . . .

> STRAUSS
>
> A simple bureaucratic procedure – his Q clearance is up for
> renewal.
> (points at Borden)
> You send your accusations to the FBI . . .

INSERT CUT: BORDEN PULLS PAPER FROM HIS TYPEWRITER. HE
SEALS AN ENVELOPE . . .

> STRAUSS
>
> Hoover sends them to the AEC . . .
> (points at Nichols)
> You're <u>forced</u> to act. You write up an indictment . . .

INT. FRONT HALL, STRAUSS RESIDENCE – NIGHT (B&W)

Strauss opens the door to Oppenheimer . . .

> STRAUSS
> (V.O.)
> Tell Oppenheimer his security clearance is not being
> renewed . . .

INT. LIVING ROOM, STRAUSS HOUSE – NIGHT (B&W)

Nichols hands the indictment to Oppenheimer, who sits and
reads. Strauss hands Oppenheimer a drink . . .

> STRAUSS
> (V.O.)
> But offer him the chance to appeal.

Oppenheimer looks up from the letter.

> OPPENHEIMER
> Can I keep this?

                         NICHOLS
No.

                         STRAUSS
As you can see, Robert, it's not yet signed. If you do decide
to appeal, they'll have to send you a copy . . .

Oppenheimer rises. In a daze. Strauss takes his arm . . .

INT. NICHOLS' OFFICE, ATOMIC ENERGY
COMMISSION – NIGHT (B&W)

                         STRAUSS
When he appeals, I appoint a board . . .

INSERT CUT: THE GRAY BOARD TAKE THEIR SEATS IN ROOM
2022 . . .

                         STRAUSS
They will, of course, have counsel –

INSERT CUT: ROGER ROBB TAKES HIS SEAT . . .

                         NICHOLS
A prosecutor?

                         STRAUSS
In all but name.

                         NICHOLS
Who?

                         STRAUSS
Roger Robb.

                         NICHOLS
Ouch.

                         STRAUSS
Robb will have security clearance to examine
Oppenheimer's file . . .

INSERT CUT: ROBB OPENS A MASSIVE BLACK BINDER . . .

                    STRAUSS
        As will the Gray Board . . .

INSERT CUT: A BLACK BINDER IS PLACED IN FRONT OF EACH
BOARD MEMBER . . .

                    STRAUSS
        Defence counsel will not.

INSERT CUT: GARRISON, AT HIS TABLE IN ROOM 2022, LOOKS
COVETOUSLY AT THE BLACK BINDERS GRACING EACH PLACE BUT
HIS . . .

                    STRAUSS
        A closed hearing – no audience, no reporters, no burden of
        proof.

                    NICHOLS
        No burden of proof?

Strauss sips his drink. Smiles at Nichols . . .

                    STRAUSS
        We're not convicting, just denying.

INT. ROOM 2022, ATOMIC ENERGY COMMISSION –
DAY (B&W)

Oppenheimer is seated at the witness table . . .

                    OPPENHEIMER
        This answer is a summary of relevant aspects of my life in
        more or less chronological order . . .

INT. SENATE OFFICE – DAY (B&W)

The Senate Aide looks like he ate a bad nut.

                    STRAUSS
        What is it you said? 'This is just how it's done'?

                    SENATE AIDE
        Forgive my naïveté.

STRAUSS

Amateurs seek the sun and get eaten, power stays in the shadows.

SENATE AIDE
(points to Time *magazine)*
You're out of the shadows, now.

STRAUSS

That's why this has to work.

SENATE AIDE
Well, Teller's testifying this morning – that'll help, then Hill is in the afternoon.

STRAUSS

Hill should help us, too.

Cut to:

Close on: a LETTER – AEC letterhead – 'DEAR DR OPPENHEIMER . . .'

STRAUSS
(O.S.)
As you can see, it's not yet signed . . .

INT. LIVING ROOM, STRAUSS HOUSE – LATER (COLOUR)

I look up from Nichols' letter – SHELL-SHOCKED.

STRAUSS
If you do decide to appeal, they'll have to send you a copy . . .

I hand the letter back to Nichols. Strauss takes my arm . . .

EXT. STRAUSS HOUSE – CONTINUOUS

Strauss gently guides me down the steps . . .

                    STRAUSS
Take my car and driver. I insist.

                    OPPENHEIMER
I'll have to consult my lawyers.

                    STRAUSS
Of course. But don't take too long, I can't keep Nichols at
bay. I'm sorry it's come to this, Robert.

Strauss, like a parent, puts me into the back of his car.

INT. STRAUSS CAR – NIGHT

I sit in the back, shadows flicking across my face . . .

                    OPPENHEIMER
                      (V.O.)
Nichols wants me to fight so that he can get it all in the
record . . .

INT. VOLPE'S HOUSE – NIGHT

Kitty and I sit with Joe Volpe.

                    OPPENHEIMER
Strauss thinks I should walk away . . .

                    VOLPE
You could. Your security clearance expires tomorrow. Just
let it go.

                    KITTY
You'd be accepting the charges! You'll lose your job. Your
reputation, your place in history! We'll lose our house.
Robert, we have to fight.

I look at Kitty. Nod.

                    VOLPE
As AEC Counsel, I can't represent you. I'll call Lloyd
Garrison.

OPPENHEIMER
He's good.

                              VOLPE
The best. But I have to warn you . . .

INT. ROOM 2022, ATOMIC ENERGY COMMISSION –
DAY

I watch Garrison scramble to make notes . . .

                              VOLPE
                              (V.O.)
This won't be a fair fight.

                              ROBB
During your interview with Boris Pash in 1943, did you
refer to microfilm?

                          OPPENHEIMER
No.

Robb consults a paper in his black binder.

                              ROBB
You never said 'a man at the consulate expert in the use of
microfilm'?

                          OPPENHEIMER
Not specifically.

                            GARRISON
I'd like to know what document Mr Robb is quoting from,
and if we might be furnished with a copy.

                              ROBB
The document is classified.

                            GARRISON
Members of the board, we're now hearing some new
account of the interview . . . shouldn't we get back to first-
hand information?

ROBB

This *is* first-hand.

GARRISON

How so?

Robb looks at Gray. Who nods.

ROBB

There's a recording of the interview.

Garrison is shocked. I shake my head.

GARRISON

You've let my client sit up here and potentially perjure himself and all this time you had a recording – ?

ROBB

No one told your client to misrepresent his former answers –

GARRISON

Misrepresent? It was twelve years ago!
                    (to the board)
Can we listen to this recording?

ROBB

Mr Garrison, you don't have clearance.

I SNAP at the absurdity –

OPPENHEIMER

But you're reading it into the transcript!

Garrison puts a calming hand on my arm –

GARRISON

Is this proceeding interested in truth or entrapment? Because if it's truth . . .

Garrison points at the BLACK BINDERS in front of them all –

GARRISON

Where's the disclosure? Where's the witness list?

                                GRAY

Mr Garrison, this is not a trial – as you're well aware.
Evidentiary rules do not apply. We're dealing with national
security.

                              GARRISON

How does national security prevent the prosecution from
providing us a list of witnesses?!

Gray looks at Garrison, stony-faced.

                                GRAY

Perhaps a brief recess is in order.

                            OPPENHEIMER

If I may? You gentlemen have my words. If you say it's
from a transcript then I'll accept it. I've already explained
that I made up a cock-and-bull story.

                                ROBB

But not the level of detail. Why would anyone present such
an elabourate fiction?

                            OPPENHEIMER

Because I was an idiot. I found myself trying to give a tip
to the intelligence people, without realizing that when
you give a tip you have to offer the whole story. Asked
for details, I went off on a false pattern. There was no
microfilm, no consular attaché. There weren't three or
more people involved on the project. There was one person
involved. That was me.

                                ROBB

Why lie?

                            OPPENHEIMER

Clearly with the intention of not revealing who was the
intermediary.

                                ROBB

Your friend, Haakon Chevalier. The Communist.

OPPENHEIMER

Yes.

ROBB

Is he still your friend?

I look from smug Robb to the expectant board members . . .

OPPENHEIMER

Chevalier is my friend.

Robb backs down, SATISFIED.

INT. CORRIDOR OUTSIDE ROOM 2022 – DAY

Oppenheimer and Garrison take a break. Rabi approaches.

GARRISON

Dr Rabi, thanks for coming.

Garrison looks around to see Robb conferring with his team.

GARRISON
(lowered voice)
Do you know anyone the prosecution has called?

RABI

Teller, obviously.
(looks at Oppenheimer)
They've asked Lawrence.

OPPENHEIMER

What did he say?

RABI

He wasn't going to help them . . .

OPPENHEIMER

But?

RABI

Strauss told him that you and Ruth Tolman had been
having an affair for years. The whole time you lived with
them in Pasadena . . .

INSERT CUT: I SIP FROM RUTH'S DRINK AT THE CHRISTMAS
PARTY. RICHARD ENTERS, BANGING SNOW OFF HIS
SHOULDERS . . .

> RABI
>
> He convinced Lawrence that Richard died of a broken
> heart.

> OPPENHEIMER
>
> That's absurd.

> RABI
>
> Which part?

> OPPENHEIMER
>
> The broken heart. Richard never found out.

Rabi tries not to smile. Shakes his head.

> OPPENHEIMER
>
> Is Lawrence going to testify?

> RABI
>
> I don't know.

INT. ROOM 2022, ATOMIC ENERGY COMMISSION –
DAY

Rabi is testifying.

> GARRISON
>
> Dr Rabi, what governmental positions do you currently
> hold?

> RABI
>
> I'm Chairman of the General Advisory Committee to the
> AEC, succeeding Dr Oppenheimer.

> GARRISON
>
> And how long have you known Dr Oppenheimer?

> RABI
>
> Since 1928. I know him quite well.

                              GARRISON

Well enough to speak on the bearing of his character,
loyalty and associations?

                              RABI

Dr Oppenheimer is a man of upstanding character, loyal
to the United States, to his friends and to the institutions
of which he is a part. I've examined his security file,
and in spite of the associations in there, I do not believe
Dr Oppenheimer is a security risk, and that these
associations from the past should bar him from continuing
as a consultant to the AEC.

EXT. CORRIDOR OUTSIDE ROOM 2022 – DAY

I sit, exhausted. A segment of orange drops into my lap –

                              RABI
        Eat.

I 'sip' at the orange. Rabi spots Lawrence coming down the
corridor – Rabi straightens to his full height – STARES DOWN
Lawrence, who looks from Rabi to me. Then TURNS and leaves.

                           OPPENHEIMER
        What was that?

                              RABI
        Nothing to worry about.

INT. ROOM 2022, ATOMIC ENERGY COMMISSION –
LATER

Robb cross-examines Rabi –

                              ROBB
Dr Rabi, after the Russian A-bomb test, did Dr Lawrence
come to see you prior to the GAC meeting?

                              RABI
You'd be better off asking him.

ROBB

I fully intend to. Did he come to you about the Hydrogen bomb?

RABI

Yes. We all felt that after the Russian explosion we had to do something to regain our position.

ROBB

So you agreed with those who felt we should launch a programme for the Super at that time?

RABI

No. There were all kinds of legitimate concerns about the allocation of our resources.

GRAY

Would you say Dr Oppenheimer was unalterably opposed to the H-bomb?

RABI

No. He thought a fusion programme would come at the expense of our awfully good fission programme.

ROBB

But that proved not to be the case?

RABI

In the event, both could be done. Los Alamos, which Dr Oppenheimer founded, rose to the occasion and worked miracles, absolute miracles.

ROBB

May I ask one more question? A purely hypothetical question. Suppose this board should not be satisfied that in his testimony here Dr Oppenheimer had told the whole truth . . . What would you say then about whether or not he ought to be cleared?

RABI

If you want to set me up on the board, then I'll give you an answer. But I've never hidden my opinion that I think this whole proceeding is a most unfortunate one.

ROBB

Why?

RABI

He's a consultant – you don't want to consult the guy? Don't. Why go through all this against a man who's accomplished what Dr Oppenheimer has? Look at his record – we have an A-bomb and a whole series of it, and we have a whole series of Super bombs and what more do you want, mermaids?

Cut to:

INT. SENATE COMMITTEE HEARING ROOM – DAY
(B & W)

Strauss watches with satisfaction as Teller testifies.

TELLER

. . . that's why I'm here today. To express the warm support for science and scientists Mr Strauss has shown over the years I've known him.

CHAIRMAN

Thank you, Dr Teller. We'll break now, unless there's any immediate business.

STRAUSS

Senator, I'd like to once again request that we're furnished with a list of witnesses.

CHAIRMAN

And I'll remind the nominee that we don't always have that information in advance. We do know that Dr Hill will be here after lunch.

With that, the Chairman BANGS *his gavel . . .*

Cut to:

INT. ROOM 2022, ATOMIC ENERGY COMMISSION –
DAY (COLOUR)

Robb addresses the board . . .

> ROBB
> Our next scheduled witness, Dr Lawrence, has apparently
> come down with . . . colitis . . .

I glance sideways at Garrison, who almost smiles –

> ROBB
> So I'll proceed instead with William Borden.

I watch as Borden is sworn in.

> ROBB
> Mr Borden, as a result of your study of Dr Oppenheimer,
> did you reach certain conclusions?

> BORDEN
> I did.

> ROBB
> Did there come a time when you expressed those
> conclusions in a letter to Mr J. Edgar Hoover of the
> Federal Bureau of Investigation?

> BORDEN
> That is correct.

> ROBB
> Prior to writing that letter, did you discuss the writing
> of it with anybody connected with the Atomic Energy
> Commission?

> BORDEN
> I did not.

> ROBB
> Do you have a copy of the letter with you?

Robb's assistant distributes copies of the letter . . .

> BORDEN
> I have one in front of me.

> ROBB
> Would you be good enough to read it?

> GARRISON
> A moment, please!

Garrison holds up a finger, FRANTICALLY reading ahead –

> GRAY
> What's the purpose of the delay? He's simply going to read this.

> GARRISON
> Mr Chairman, this is the first we've seen of this letter – and I see statements, at least one, which I don't think anybody would be happy to have go into the record – accusations that have not before been made and are not part of the indictment from Nichols.

Garrison holds up the letter –

> GARRISON
> Is it the opinion of the board that these are matters into which inquiry should now be directed?

I scan down the letter for what he's seen. My face falls . . .

> GRAY
> Testimony of this witness is not in any way going to broaden the inquiry.

> GARRISON
> How can it avoid it, sir? Supposing you should believe the witness? Mr Robb is tasked by this board with calling in witnesses, and he brings in one to make accusations of a kind that I don't think belong here.

Mr Chairman, the witness wrote this letter on his own initiative laying out evidence which has already been before the board. His conclusions are valid testimony just like the positive conclusions of friends of Dr Oppenheimer. It cuts both ways.

GARRISON

How long has counsel been in possession of the letter?

ROBB

Mr Garrison, I don't think I should be subject to cross-examination by you.

GRAY

Mr Garrison, given that we on the board have all read the letter, isn't it better to have it in the record?

Garrison says nothing. He looks at me, frustrated.

GRAY

Let's proceed.

BORDEN

'Dear Mr Hoover, the purpose of this letter is to state my opinion, based upon years of study of the available classified evidence, that more probably than not J. Robert Oppenheimer is an agent of the Soviet Union.'

I turn the letter face down, staring at its blank whiteness . . .

BORDEN

'The following conclusions are justified. One: Between 1929 and 1942, more probably than not, J. Robert Oppenheimer was a sufficiently hardened Communist that he volunteered information to the Soviets. Two: More probably than not, he has since been functioning as an espionage agent.'

I watch the STENOGRAPHER calmly type this into the record . . .

'Three: More probably than not, he has since acted under a Soviet directive in influencing United States military, atomic energy, intelligence, and diplomatic policy.'

Devastated, I cannot meet the eye of anyone in the room. Garrison gets up from his place. Sits down next to me.

GARRISON

I'm sorry, Robert.

OPPENHEIMER

Isn't anyone ever going to tell the truth about what's happening here?

Cut to:

INT. SENATE COMMITTEE HEARING ROOM – DAY (B&W)

Strauss and his Counsel take their seats as the Chairman calls to order. Strauss looks around the room, CHEERFULLY.

CHAIRMAN

We will now hear from Dr David Hill.

Strauss peers at a FAMILIAR man in GLASSES, DAVID HILL – Szilard's note-taking scientist WHOSE PEN OPPENHEIMER GRABBED . . .

CHAIRMAN

Dr Hill, would you care to make a statement?

HILL

Thank you. I have been asked to testify about Lewis Strauss, a man who has given years of service in high positions of government and who is known to be earnest, hard-working and intelligent.

Strauss glances at Counsel, satisfied.

*The views I have to express are my own, but I believe
that much I have to say will help indicate why most of the
scientists in this country would prefer to see Mr Strauss
completely out of the government.*

Strauss narrows his eyes . . .

SENATOR PASTORE
(friendly lob)
*You're referring to the hostility of certain scientists directed
at Mr Strauss because of his commitment to security, as
demonstrated in the Oppenheimer affair?*

HILL

No.

Hill takes a sip of water before continuing . . .

HILL
*Because of the personal vindictiveness he demonstrated
against Dr Oppenheimer, and against all those who have
disagreed with his official positions.*

Counsel turns to Strauss, who is FIXATED on Hill. The
Senate Aide REACTS, surprised. MURMURS echo through the
chamber . . .

HILL
*In my ten years observation of Mr Strauss I have seen
his incapacity to change a position, the subordination of
his integrity to the attainment of political goals and an
obsessive quest for popular and professional approval . . .*

The audience REACTS – Strauss SHAKES his head – the Chairman
BANGS the gavel –

CHAIRMAN

Order!

Cut to:

INT. ROOM 2022, ATOMIC ENERGY COMMISSION – DAY (COLOUR)

Vannevar Bush is sworn in.

> BUSH
> It appears to most scientists around the country that Oppenheimer is now being pilloried and put through an ordeal because he expressed his honest opinions. The written charges against him are in a poorly written indictment which the board should have rejected from the outset.

> EVANS
> Dr Bush, I thought I was performing a service to my country in hearing this case.

> BUSH
> No board in this country should sit in judgement of a man because he expressed strong opinions. If you want to try that case, you can try me – I have expressed strong opinions, often unpopular, many times. I'm doing so right now. When a man is pilloried for doing that, this country is in a severe state . . . excuse me, gentlemen, if I become stirred, but I am.

Cut to:

INT. SENATE COMMITTEE HEARING ROOM – DAY (B&W)

Strauss fumes as Hill reads his statement.

> HILL
> *From the standpoint of public welfare, the most injurious exercise of personal vindictiveness in which Lewis Strauss has engaged was in the personnel security prosecution of J. Robert Oppenheimer, who had not hesitated to disagree with Mr Strauss on certain questions of fundamental policy. Oppenheimer made mincemeat out of Strauss'*

*position on the shipments of isotopes to Norway, and
Strauss never forgave him this public humiliation.
Another controversy between them centreed around
their differences in judgement on how the H-bomb
would contribute to national security. Oppenheimer had
considerable influence and prestige, and Strauss was able
to find a few ambitious men who also disagreed with
Oppenheimer's position, and envied him his prestige in
government circles.*

Teller, in the audience, stares at Hill . . .

HILL
*Strauss turned to the personnel security system in order to
destroy Oppenheimer's effectiveness –*

SENATOR PASTORE
*But, Dr Hill, we've already heard that Mr Strauss did not
bring the charges, or participate in the hearings against
Dr Oppenheimer.*

HILL
*I realize that Mr Strauss didn't sign the letter of charges,
but I think when all of the evidence is viewed, it becomes
highly plausible that the Oppenheimer matter was initiated
and carried through largely through the animus of Lewis
Strauss.*

Cut to:

INT. ROOM 2022, ATOMIC ENERGY COMMISSION –
DAY (COLOUR)

Groves is testifying.

ROBB
General, would you clear Dr Oppenheimer today?

GROVES
Under my interpretation of the Atomic Energy Act, which
did not exist when I hired Dr Oppenheimer in 1942 . . .

I would not clear Dr Oppenheimer today if I were a member of the commission.

ROBB

Thank you, General.

GROVES

But I'm not sure I could've cleared *any* of those guys.

ROBB

That's all.

GARRISON

General, Dr Oppenheimer had no responsibility for the selection or clearance of Klaus Fuchs, did he?

GROVES

No, not at all.

GARRISON

You wouldn't want to leave with this board even the remotest suggestion that you're here questioning Dr Oppenheimer's basic loyalty to the United States in the operation of Los Alamos?

GROVES

By no means. I hope I didn't lead anybody to think otherwise for an instant.

GARRISON

Would you say that the revocation of Dr Oppenheimer's position would be in the public interest?

GROVES

The revocation under such extreme publicity I think would be most unfortunate, not because of the effect on Dr Oppenheimer – that I leave to one side – but because of the disastrous effect upon the attitude of the scientists of this country toward doing government research.

GRAY

Thank you, General.

Groves gets up, walks past me with a formal nod.

INT. CORRIDOR OUTSIDE ROOM 2022 – DAY

Garrison checks his watch.

> OPPENHEIMER
> She'll be here.

> GARRISON
> Do you even want her here?

> OPPENHEIMER
> Only a fool or an adolescent presumes to know someone else's relationship, and you're neither, Lloyd.

Kitty comes around the corner. Unsteady. I watch her walk towards us, not entirely straight . . . she catches my eye –

> OPPENHEIMER
> Kitty and I, we're grown-ups. We've walked through fire together. And she'll do fine.

INT. ROOM 2022, ATOMIC ENERGY COMMISSION – DAY

Kitty is at the witness table. From behind I can see her fiddling distractedly with her purse . . .

> GARRISON
> Mrs Oppenheimer, you are no longer a member of the Communist Party?

> KITTY
> No.

> GARRISON
> When would you say that you ceased to be a member?

> KITTY
> When I left Youngstown in 1936.

> GARRISON
> Will you describe your views on Communism as pro, anti, neutral.

                              KITTY
Very strongly against. I've had nothing to do with
Communism since 1936. Since before I met Robert.

                            GARRISON
That's all.

                              HILL
                             (V.O.)
The record demonstrates that Oppenheimer was not
interrogated by impartial and disinterested counsel for the
Gray Board . . .

Robb gets up to cross-examine . . .

Cut to:

INT. SENATE COMMITTEE HEARING ROOM – DAY
(B&W)

Strauss watches Hill continue to answer questions . . .

                              HILL
*. . . he was interrogated by a prosecutor who used all the
tricks of a rather ingenious legal background to try to
trick Oppenheimer into erroneous statements, and he did
succeed in a few instances.*

                         SENATOR SCOTT
*You are charging now that the Gray Board permitted a
prosecution of Dr Oppenheimer. Do you think, then, that
the members of the Gray Board were unfair?*

Hill takes a beat to consider this.

                              HILL
*I can only say if I'd been on the Gray Board, I would've
protested against the tactics of the man who served in fact
as a prosecuting counsel – a man appointed not by the
board but by Lewis Strauss.*

Strauss strokes his chin, feigning indifference.

SENATOR McGEE

Who was this?

Cut to:

INT. ROOM 2022, ATOMIC ENERGY COMMISSION –
DAY (COLOUR)

                    HILL
                   (V.O.)
Roger Robb.

Robb tries to put himself in Kitty's eyeline . . .

                    ROBB
    Mrs Oppenheimer.

She will not meet his gaze.

                    ROBB
    Did you have a Communist Party membership card?

                    KITTY
    I, I'm not sure . . .

Kitty fiddles with her purse . . .

                    ROBB
    Not sure?

                    KITTY
    Well . . .

She FREEZES. The Board members look at her. Garrison looks at me . . .

                    ROBB
    Presumably the act of joining the Party was sending some
    money and receiving a card?

Kitty is focused on her purse . . .

                    ROBB
    No?

And then Kitty LOOKS UP at Robb, pure STEEL –

> KITTY
> It was all just so long ago, Mr Robb, wasn't it?

> ROBB
> Not really –

> KITTY
> Long enough to have forgotten.

> ROBB
> Did you turn in the card or rip it up?

> KITTY
> The card whose existence I've forgotten?

> ROBB
> Your Communist Party membership card –

> KITTY
> I haven't the slightest idea.

> ROBB
> Can a distinction be made between Soviet Communism and Communism?

> KITTY
> In the days when I was a member I thought they were definitely two things –

Garrison and I hang on her every word . . .

> KITTY
> I thought the Communist Party of the United States was concerned with our domestic problems. I now no longer believe this. I believe the whole thing is linked together and spread all over the world. I've believed this since I left the Party sixteen years ago.

> ROBB
> But –

> KITTY
> Seventeen years ago. My mistake.

ROBB

But you –

KITTY

Sorry, eighteen. Yes, eighteen years ago.

Robb sighs patiently.

ROBB

Were you familiar with the fact that your husband was making contributions to the Spanish Civil War as late as 1942?

KITTY

I knew that Robert gave money from time to time, yes.

ROBB

Do you remember whether he gave money on a regular or periodic basis?

Kitty smiles sweetly –

KITTY

Do you mean regular, or do you mean periodic, Mr Robb?

ROBB
(annoyed)

I mean . . . regular.

KITTY

He did not.

ROBB

Were you aware that this money was going into Communist Party channels?

KITTY

Don't you mean 'through'?

ROBB

Pardon?

KITTY

I think you mean 'through Communist Party channels'.

ROBB

Yes.

KITTY

Yes.

ROBB

Would it be fair to say that this meant that by 1942 he had not stopped having anything to do with the Communist Party? I don't insist that you answer yes or no. You can answer any way you wish.

KITTY

I know that. Thank you. But the question isn't properly phrased.

ROBB

Do you understand what I am trying to get at?

KITTY

Yes, I do.

ROBB

Why don't you answer it that way?

KITTY

I don't like the phrase 'having anything to do with the Communist Party' because Robert never had anything to do with the Communist Party as such. I know he gave money for Spanish refugees. I know he took an intellectual interest in Communist ideas –

ROBB

Are there two kinds of Communists? An intellectual Communist and a plain ordinary Commie?

Kitty laughs the laugh of the free.

KITTY

I couldn't answer that one.

EVANS
(delighted)

I couldn't either.

Gray shoots a look at Evans. CHUCKLES around the room. Garrison looks at me. Nods. She did good.

INT. ROOM 2022, ATOMIC ENERGY COMMISSION – DAY

I watch Teller testify.

ROBB

Is it your intention to suggest that Dr Oppenheimer is disloyal to the United States?

TELLER

I do not want to suggest anything of the kind. I have always assumed, and now assume, that he is loyal to the United States. I believe this, and I shall believe it until I see very conclusive proof to the opposite.

ROBB

Now, a question which is a corollary of that . . . do you or do you not believe that Dr Oppenheimer is a security risk?

TELLER

In a great number of cases I have seen Dr Oppenheimer act in a way which for me was exceedingly hard to understand. I thoroughly disagreed with him in numerous issues, and his actions, frankly, appeared to me confused and complicated. To this extent, I feel that I would like to see the vital interests of this country in hands which I understand better and therefore trust more.

GRAY

Thank you, doctor.

Teller gets up from the table, as he walks past me he holds out his hand . . .

TELLER

I'm sorry.

I shake his hand.

KITTY
(V.O.)
You shook his fucking hand?!

INT. DINING ROOM, OLDEN MANOR, PRINCETON –
NIGHT

KITTY
I would've spat in his face!

GARRISON
I'm not sure the board would've appreciated that.

KITTY
Not gentlemanly enough? You're all being too goddamn
gentlemanly.

VOLPE
Gray must see what Robb is doing – why doesn't he shut
him down?

Garrison shrugs.

KITTY
(to me)
And you? Shaking Teller's hand – you need to stop playing
the martyr.

EXT. OLDEN MANOR, PRINCETON – NIGHT

Garrison drives off. Volpe turns to me –

VOLPE
Robert, you can't win this thing. It's a kangaroo court with
a predetermined outcome. Why put yourself through more
of it?

OPPENHEIMER
I have my reasons.

Volpe shrugs. Embraces me. Gets in his car.

EINSTEIN
(O.S.)
He has a point, you know.

I turn. Einstein steps into the light.

EINSTEIN
You're a man chasing a woman who doesn't love him any
more – the United States Government.

OPPENHEIMER
I'm not sure you understand, Albert.

EINSTEIN
No? I left my country, never to return. The German
calamity of years ago repeats itself – people acquiesce
without resistance and align themselves with the forces of
evil. You've served America well, and if this is the reward
she has to offer perhaps you should turn your back on her.

OPPENHEIMER
Dammit, I happen to love this country.

Einstein considers this. Nods slowly.

EINSTEIN
Then tell them to go to hell.

Cut to:

INT. SENATE OFFICE – DAY (B&W)

Strauss BURSTS in, fuming . . .

STRAUSS
This has become a trial about a trial!

205

SENATE AIDE

It's not good that he's telling them that you initiated the hearings.

STRAUSS

He can't prove it. He can't prove that I gave the file to Borden.

SENATE AIDE

He doesn't have to. We're not in court, there's no burden of proof...

Strauss realizes. Shakes his head at himself...

STRAUSS

They're not convicting. Just denying.

The Senate Aide nods.

STRAUSS

Why would Hill come here to tear me down? What's his angle?

SENATE AIDE

Do people need a reason to do the right thing?

Strauss GLARES at the Senate Aide.

SENATE AIDE

I mean, as he sees it.

STRAUSS

I told you Oppenheimer poisoned the scientists against me! Right from that first meeting...

INSERT CUT: STRAUSS WATCHES OPPENHEIMER HAND EINSTEIN HIS HAT AS THEY SPEAK DOWN AT THE LAKE...

STRAUSS

I don't know what Oppenheimer said to him that day, but Einstein wouldn't even meet my eye...

INSERT CUT: AS STRAUSS APPROACHES, EINSTEIN WALKS PAST WITHOUT ACKNOWLEDGING HIM, CLEARLY UPSET...

206

Oppenheimer knows how to manipulate his own. At Los Alamos he preyed on the naïveté of scientists who thought they'd get a say in how we used their work . . . but don't ever think he was that naive himself . . .

Cut to:

INT. ROOM 2022, ATOMIC ENERGY COMMISSION – DAY (COLOUR)

I am back at the witness table. Robb squares up.

ROBB
Doctor, in your work on the Hydrogen bomb at Los Alamos and in the years following, were you deterred by any moral qualms about the development of this weapon?

OPPENHEIMER
Of course.

ROBB
But you still got on with the work, didn't you?

OPPENHEIMER
Yes, because this was work of exploration. It was not the preparation of a weapon.

ROBB
You mean it was just an academic excursion?

OPPENHEIMER
No. It's not an academic thing whether you can make a Hydrogen bomb. It's a matter of life and death.

ROBB
Beginning in 1942 you were actively pushing the development of the H-bomb, weren't you?

OPPENHEIMER
'Pushing' is not the right word. Supporting and working on it, yes.

ROBB

When did these moral qualms become so strong that you opposed the development of the Hydrogen bomb?

OPPENHEIMER

When it was suggested that it be the policy of the United States to make these things at all costs, without regard to the balance between these weapons and atomic weapons as part of our arsenal.

ROBB
(theatrical confusion)

What did moral qualms have to do with *that*?

OPPENHEIMER
(struggling)

What did moral qualms have to do with it?

ROBB

Yes.

INT. SENATE OFFICE – DAY (B&W)

Strauss is pacing now . . .

STRAUSS

Oppenheimer wanted to own the atomic bomb. He wanted to be the man who moved the earth. He talks about putting the nuclear genie back in the bottle – well, I'm here to tell you that I know J. Robert Oppenheimer and if he could do it all over he'd do it all the same. He's never once said he regrets Hiroshima – he'd do it all over because it made him the most important man who ever lived . . .

INT. ROOM 2022, ATOMIC ENERGY COMMISSION – DAY (COLOUR)

I struggle to find an answer for Robb . . .

OPPENHEIMER

We freely used the atomic bomb.

ROBB

In fact, doctor, you assisted in selecting the target for the drop of the atomic bomb on Japan?

Now I can hear the sound of FEET STAMPING . . .

OPPENHEIMER

Yes.

ROBB

You knew, did you not, that the dropping of that atomic bomb on the target you had selected would kill or injure thousands of civilians, is that correct?

OPPENHEIMER

Not as many as turned out . . .

ROBB

How many were killed or injured?

The feet are stamping FASTER and FASTER . . .

OPPENHEIMER

Seventy thousand.

ROBB

Seventy thousand? At both Hiroshima and –

OPPENHEIMER

One hundred and ten thousand at both.

ROBB

On the day of each bombing.

OPPENHEIMER

Yes.

ROBB

And in the weeks and years after?

OPPENHEIMER

It's been put at between fifty and one hundred thousand . . .

                        ROBB
Two hundred and twenty thousand dead? At least?

I nod.

                        ROBB
Did you have moral scruples about that?

                    OPPENHEIMER
Terrible ones.

                        ROBB
But you testified the other day that the bombing of
Hiroshima was very successful?

                    OPPENHEIMER
Well, it was technically successful.

                        ROBB
Oh, technically.

                    OPPENHEIMER
It's also alleged to have helped end the war.

The stamping feet are LOUDER and FASTER . . .

                        ROBB
Would you have supported the dropping of a Hydrogen
bomb on Hiroshima?

INT. SENATE OFFICE – DAY (B&W)

Strauss TURNS *on the Senate Aide –*

                        STRAUSS
*But he wanted all the glory and none of the responsibility.
So he needed <u>absolution</u>. He needed to be a <u>martyr</u>, to
<u>suffer</u>, and take the <u>sins</u> of the world on his shoulders. To
say 'no, we cannot continue on this road' even as he knew
we'd <u>have</u> to . . .*

INT. ROOM 2022, ATOMIC ENERGY COMMISSION –
DAY (COLOUR)

I search for an answer – the FEET STAMPING ever LOUDER –

> OPPENHEIMER
> It would make no sense at all.

> ROBB
> Why?

> OPPENHEIMER
> The target is too small.

> ROBB
> Supposing there had been a target in Japan big enough
> for a thermonuclear weapon, would you have opposed
> dropping it?

> OPPENHEIMER
> This was not a problem with which I was confronted.

> ROBB
> I'm confronting you with it now, sir. Would you have
> opposed the dropping of a thermonuclear weapon on
> Japan because of moral scruples?

> OPPENHEIMER
> I believe I would, sir.

> ROBB
> Did you oppose the dropping of the atom bomb on
> Hiroshima because of moral scruples?

> OPPENHEIMER
> We set forth our –

> ROBB
> I'm asking *you* about it, not 'we'.

> OPPENHEIMER
> I set forth arguments against dropping it. But I did not
> endorse them.

INT. SENATE OFFICE – DAY (B&W)

Strauss PACES *the room,* FURIOUS –

> STRAUSS
> *He knew he'd have to be seen to suffer for what he did.* <u>*It*</u>
> <u>*was*</u> <u>*all*</u> <u>*part*</u> <u>*of*</u> <u>*his*</u> <u>*plan.*</u> *He wanted the glorious insincere*
> *guilt of the self-important to wear like a fucking crown.*
> *And I gave it to him . . .*

INT. ROOM 2022, ATOMIC ENERGY COMMISSION –
DAY (COLOUR)

Robb gets right in my face, incredulous –

> ROBB
> You mean having worked night and day for three years to
> build the bomb, you then argued it shouldn't be used?

> OPPENHEIMER
> No. I was asked by the Secretary of War what the views of
> scientists were – I gave the views against and the views for.

> ROBB
> You supported the dropping of the atom bomb on Japan,
> didn't you?

> OPPENHEIMER
> What do you mean 'support'?

> ROBB
> You helped pick the target, didn't you?

> OPPENHEIMER
> I did my job – I was not in a policy-making position at Los
> Alamos – I would have done anything that I was asked to
> do –

> ROBB
> You would have made the H-bomb, too, wouldn't you?

> OPPENHEIMER
> I couldn't.

The STAMPING breaks rhythm to become CACOPHONOUS . . .

> ROBB
> I didn't ask you that, doctor.

> OPPENHEIMER
> I would have worked on it, yes. But to run a labouratory is one thing, to advise a government is another.

THE LIGHT OF A THOUSAND SUNS POURS IN THE WINDOW . . .

> ROBB
> And the GAC report, which you co-authored, following the Russian atomic test said that a Super bomb should *never* be produced, did it not?

> OPPENHEIMER
> What we meant – what I meant – was that it would be a better world if there were no Hydrogen bombs in it.

LIGHT STABS THROUGH CRACKS IN THE WALL . . .

> ROBB
> Wouldn't the Soviets do anything to increase their military strength?

> OPPENHEIMER
> If we did it, they'd *have* to do it. Our efforts would fuel their efforts – just as it had with the atomic bomb!

PLASTER BREAKS AWAY AS LIGHT POURS INTO THE ROOM . . .
I JAM my eyes closed, MORE AND MORE EXPOSED . . .

> ROBB
> 'Just as with the atomic bomb.' Exactly. No moral scruples in 1945, plenty in 1949 . . .

The sound STOPS. The light is gone.

> GRAY
> (gentle)
> Dr Oppenheimer, when *did* your strong moral convictions develop with respect to the Hydrogen bomb?

I open my eyes, exhausted . . .

OPPENHEIMER

When it became clear to me that we would tend to use any
weapon we had.

Silence.

INT. SENATE OFFICE – DAY (B&W)

Strauss has stopped . . .

STRAUSS

*J. Robert Oppenheimer – the martyr. I gave him exactly
what he wanted. To be remembered for Trinity, not
Hiroshima, not Nagasaki. He should be thanking me.*

SENATE AIDE

Well, he's not.

*Strauss looks at the Senate Aide's neck, wondering if he could
get one hand all the way around it.*

STRAUSS
(speaking softly)
*Do you still have enough votes, or is the crowning moment
of my career about to become the most public humiliation
of my life?*

The Senate Aide looks down at his buck slip, counts his tally.

SENATE AIDE

You'll scrape through.

Strauss looks at the Senate Aide. He smiles.

STRAUSS

Then gather the press.

Cut to:

INT. ROOM 2022, ATOMIC ENERGY COMMISSION –
DAY (COLOUR)

I sit with Garrison and listen to Gray pass judgement . . .

> GRAY
> J. Robert Oppenheimer, this board, having heard testimony
> from you and many of your current and former colleagues,
> has come to the unanimous conclusion that you are a
> loyal citizen . . . However, in the light of your continuing
> associations and disregard for the security apparatus of
> this country, together with your somewhat disturbing
> conduct in relation to the Hydrogen bomb and the
> regrettable lack of candor in certain of your responses to
> this board, we have voted two to one to deny the renewal
> of your security clearance.

I barely hear the rest . . .

> GRAY
> A full written opinion, with a dissent from Mr Evans, will
> be issued to the AEC in the coming days . . .

The board rises, aides start collecting files. Still dazed, I take the
phone from Garrison –

> GARRISON
> It's Kitty.

> KITTY
> (over phone)
> Robert? Robert?

I take a breath. Not trusting my voice . . .

> OPPENHEIMER
> Don't . . . don't . . . don't . . . take in the sheets.

Cut to:

INT. SENATE OFFICE – DAY (B&W)

We hear the press gathering behind the doors. Strauss checks his tie in the mirror. Smooths his hair. The Senate Aide enters, buck slip in hand.

> STRAUSS
>
> Is it official?

> SENATE AIDE
>
> I'm afraid there were a couple of unexpected holdouts.

Strauss freezes, absorbing the impact.

> STRAUSS
>
> I'm denied?

The Senate Aide leaves him hanging for a beat.

> SENATE AIDE
>
> I'm afraid so, sir.

Strauss doesn't know what to do or where to look.

> STRAUSS
>
> Who were the holdouts?

> SENATE AIDE
>
> There were three, led by the junior senator from Massachusetts. Young guy, trying to make a name for himself. Didn't like what you did to Oppenheimer.

> STRAUSS
>
> What's his name?

The Senate Aide checks his tally . . .

> SENATE AIDE
>
> Uh . . . Kennedy. John F. Kennedy.

Cut to:

EXT. OLDEN MANOR, BACK GATE OVERLOOKING THE INSTITUTE – DAY (COLOUR)

I approach Kitty, who's been crying.

> KITTY
> Did you think if you let them tar and feather you the world would forgive you? It won't.

> OPPENHEIMER
> We'll see.

Cut to:

INT. SENATE OFFICE – DAY (B&W)

Strauss listens to the hungry press pack beyond the door. He TURNS on the Senate Aide –

> STRAUSS
> *Goddamn it! You told me I'd be fine!*

> SENATE AIDE
> *Well, I didn't have all the facts, did I?*

> STRAUSS
> *I did what was right for this country. They don't want me in the Cabinet Room? Maybe they should just invite Oppenheimer instead.*

> SENATE AIDE
> *Perhaps they will.*

> STRAUSS
> *He turned the scientists against me. One by one. Starting with Einstein. I told you about that? About Einstein, by the pond?*

The Senate Aide picks up Strauss's hat and coat . . .

> SENATE AIDE
> *You did. But, you know, sir, since nobody knows what they said to each other that day, is it possible they didn't*

talk about you at all? Is it possible they spoke about something . . .

Hands Strauss his hat and coat . . .

> SENATE AIDE
> *. . . more important?*

Strauss looks at the Senate Aide like he wants to kill him. The Senate Aide OPENS *the office door and the* FLASHBULBS EAT STRAUSS ALIVE *as we –*

Cut to:

EXT. LAKESIDE, INSTITUTE FOR ADVANCED STUDY, PRINCETON – DAY (COLOUR)

I approach the figure by the lake. The figure's hat BLOWS off, releasing a mass of GREY CURLS. Strauss watches from the doorway as I SCOOP up Einstein's hat . . .

> EINSTEIN
> Robert. The man of the moment.

I hand him his hat. He looks out at the lake.

> EINSTEIN
> You once had a reception for me at Berkeley. Gave me an award. You all believed I'd lost the ability to understand what I'd started. So that award wasn't for me . . . it was for all of you.

Einstein turns to me.

> EINSTEIN
> Now it's your turn to deal with the consequences of your achievements. And one day . . . when they've punished you enough . . .

INT. CABINET ROOM, WHITE HOUSE – DAY

Dozens of formally attired GUESTS. Kitty by my side. Many faces, now older, are there – Rabi, Lawrence, Frank, Jackie . . .

                    EINSTEIN
                     (V.O.)
They'll serve salmon and potato salad, make speeches, give you a medal . . .

LYNDON JOHNSON places a MEDAL around my neck. I SMILE and shake the President's hand. Kitty BEAMS as she, in turn, shakes Johnson's hand . . . Frank comes up to me, gives me a quick embrace –

                     FRANK
You're happy, I'm happy . . .

                  OPPENHEIMER
Then I'm happy you're happy.

Lawrence claps me on the shoulder, smiling affectionately . . .

                    EINSTEIN
                     (V.O.)
Pat you on the back and tell you all is forgiven . . .

Teller approaches, I smile and take his offered hand . . .

                    EINSTEIN
                     (V.O.)
Just remember. It won't be for you . . .

Teller turns to Kitty, offering the same smile and handshake . . .

                    EINSTEIN
                     (V.O.)
. . . it'll be for them.

Kitty STARES Teller down, letting his hand hang in the air like a WILTING PLANT . . . and we –

Cut to:

EXT. LAKESIDE, INSTITUTE FOR ADVANCED STUDY, PRINCETON – DAY

Einstein TURNS to leave. Up the hill, Strauss approaches . . .

> OPPENHEIMER
> Albert? When I came to you with those calculations?

Einstein pauses. I watch raindrops make circles on the surface of the pond . . .

> OPPENHEIMER
> We were worried that we'd start a chain reaction that would destroy the entire world . . .

> EINSTEIN
> I remember it well. What of it?

> OPPENHEIMER
> I believe we did.

Einstein PALES. TURNS, passing Strauss without a word . . . The sound of FEET STAMPING . . .

Close in on: my staring eyes as I visualize THE EXPANDING NUCLEAR ARSENALS OF THE WORLD . . . THE FEET, FASTER AND FASTER –

When I can take it no longer, I JAM my eyes CLOSED and we –

Cut to black.

Credits.

End.

Printed in the USA
CPSIA information can be obtained
at www.ICGtesting.com
JSHW021056160823
46500JS00010B/10